MASTER YOUR BELIEFS

A PRACTICAL GUIDE TO STOP DOUBTING
YOURSELF AND BUILD UNSHAKEABLE
CONFIDENCE

THIBAUT MEURISSE

Edited by
KERRY J DONOVAN

CONTENTS

Are you tired of seeing everyone moving ahead in life while you remain stuck in an unsatisfying career or relationship? Are you sick of being told to "be more confident" without ever knowing how to do it? Do you feel as though life is passing you by while you remain insecure and unable to develop the confidence to pursue the goals you want?

If you want to discover a specific method to develop unshakeable self-belief so that you can finally go after the things you really want, this book is for you.

In this book, you will learn:

- What belief is and how exactly it works,
- Why anyone can become confident and how to do it,
- The seven core beliefs that will skyrocket your confidence,
- How to use the power of belief to achieve almost anything you desire,
- The Belief Formula that will explode your confidence, and
- How to sustain high level confidence over the long term and develop unshakeable determination.

If any of the above resonates with you, read on.

WHY THIS BOOK

Your ability to believe is one of the most powerful tools you have. Once you believe something is possible, you will begin to take action and will not stop until your vision becomes a reality. In other words, the simple act of *believing* creates the necessary conditions for the attainment of any goals or dreams. On the other hand, when you're full of doubt, not believing something is within your reach, you probably won't even take the first step in that direction.

Unfortunately, you've never been taught how to believe, and neither was I. You weren't offered a *Belief 101 Course* at school. Instead, you were left alone to figure it out all by yourself, assuming you even realized you had such an incredible gift called "belief" inside you. Using this belief, you can explore almost unlimited possibilities and achieve seemingly impossible things.

For the most part, what you believe determines what you can (or cannot) accomplish in your life. This is why having a solid understanding of how belief works is critical. In this book, you'll discover how belief works and you will learn a specific formula that will enable you to develop rock-solid confidence. I invite you to see this book as a practical guide to building greater confidence. Refer to it as often as necessary.

My sincere hope is that, by using the exercises detailed in this book, you will give yourself full permission to use the power of belief to achieve your most ambitious goals and live the life you want—the life you deserve.

INTRODUCTION

There is something in this world that cannot be touched nor seen. It has no smell, form or shape, yet it is one of the most powerful forces on earth. It is a force that influences people and leads to unbelievable transformations and mind-blowing innovations. And this thing isn't just for the elite. It's accessible to everyone. In fact, it is the very thing that differentiates human beings from any other species on earth.

This extraordinary power is ...

belief.

Belief is the intangible thing that makes the tangible possible. It is the source of human creation. In fact, every human-made item is the result of a thought in someone's mind; a thought that was energized enough to be acted upon and created in the real world.

The ability to believe has been within you all along, but you may have neglected it, forgotten about it or misunderstood it. Now is the time to reclaim it. As you practice using the power of belief, you'll be able to change yourself and the world around you far beyond anything you imagined was possible.

In this book, we'll dive deep into the nature of belief and explain why it is critical for you to understand its very fabric. We'll see how you can use your in-built belief not only to transform your own life but also to serve others around you.

In **PART I.** *The nature of belief*, we'll explore in depth what belief is and why it's critical to your success. We'll see that believing is a skill accessible to everyone and that you can use it to "distort" reality.

In **PART II.** *Identifying your limiting beliefs*, we'll work on identifying your current beliefs. We'll uncover the limiting beliefs that hold you back, and we'll see what you can do to start eliminating them so you can finally reach your true potential.

In **PART III.** *Building fundamental beliefs*, we'll learn the core beliefs necessary to reconstruct your model of reality. Armed with new empowering beliefs, you'll be well on your way to developing rock-solid confidence.

In **PART IV.** *The Belief Formula*, we'll explore the key components required to develop unshakeable confidence. You'll discover that you can develop belief by following a specific formula that anyone can apply. Furthermore, as you apply this formula, your confidence will inevitably grow.

Finally, in **PART V.** *Sustaining belief long term*, we'll discuss how to maintain rock-solid belief over a long period of time so that you can achieve whatever goal you desire.

By reading to the end of this book, you'll have all the tools you need to eliminate self-doubt and develop rock-solid confidence.

So, are you ready to uncover the power of belief, develop unshakeable confidence and explode your results?

Master Your Life With The Mastery Series

This book is the seventh book in the *Mastery Series*. You can check out the first book, *Master Your Emotions* at the URL below:

http://mybook.to/Master_Emotions

What readers say about *Master Your Emotions*:

"I am a psychologist and I love this book because of it's simplicity. It is so easy to read and understand. I will be referring many of my clients to download this book." -- Laura Beth Cooper, Ph.D., Psychologist

"Changed my life"

"This book kept me all the way to the end! I couldn't put it down and when I did I couldn't wait to pick it up again!"

"One of the best self help books I have ever read!"

"This will be one of my go to books, like How to Win Friends and Influence People, Start with Why, and a handful of others that I will continuously go back to."

PART I

THE NATURE OF BELIEF

The mind is such a powerful instrument; it can deliver to you literally everything you want. But you first have to believe that what you want is possible. And belief is a choice. It is simply a thought you choose to think over and over until it becomes automatic.

— JACK CANFIELD, AUTHOR AND MOTIVATIONAL SPEAKER.

Have you ever considered what belief is at its core? Could you explain why one person is able to believe in his or her goals and make them a reality while others are crippled by self-doubt and unable to press forward? After all, belief is not something tangible. So, why are some people able to believe while others can't?

In this section, we'll explore this question and others. We'll look in depth at what belief is so that you begin to understand how it works and how you can develop more of it.

Note that in this book I will use the words, "self-belief", "self-confidence", and "confidence" interchangeably as they are largely synonymous and cover the same concept.

I will also use the expression "the power of belief" many times, which refers to our innate ability to keep believing in something and to keep taking the action necessary to make it happen. This ability is what separates us from every other living creature on earth. It is the superpower that allows us to think of something—physical object or idea—and to "create" it in the real world.

Now, let's discuss what belief is and how it works.

1

WHAT BELIEF IS

Put simply, belief is the ability to put enough focus and energy into an idea so that it influences your behavior—whether consciously or unconsciously. In this regard, we must differentiate "believing" from "thinking".

Thinking is an activity you engage in all day long, but it doesn't necessarily lead to action or impact upon your behavior. Considering you have thousands of thoughts every day, it is fortunate you don't have to act on each one of them. For instance, if you have a thought that you'd like to travel to France, it doesn't mean you're going to act on that thought instantly. And if the thought, "I wouldn't mind eating a donut" crosses your mind, that doesn't mean you'll stop everything to go buy that donut.

Conversely, belief is much more powerful than mere thought. Your beliefs are more deeply rooted in your mind. They dictate how you perceive yourself and the world around you, and they directly impact your decisions. Below are some ways belief may affect your behavior:

- If you believe you aren't very smart, you will probably not pursue your biggest dreams,
- If you believe you're shy, you might not engage in certain

activities you perceive as impossible for you (e.g., giving a speech, approaching someone at an event, et cetera), and
- If you believe money is evil, you probably won't make much of it or will quickly get rid of any money you earn.

Fortunately, your beliefs do not represent reality. You can replace your disempowering beliefs with more empowering ones, which we will cover in **PART II.** *Identifying your limiting beliefs.*

1. The connection between belief and thought

Even though thoughts and beliefs are different, they are nevertheless interconnected and feed each other:

- Thoughts crystallize into beliefs when they are given enough attention over time, and
- Beliefs generate thoughts, which further strengthen those beliefs

If you keep thinking a specific thought, you'll begin to form the corresponding belief. For instance, if you repeatedly tell yourself that you are the most tenacious person you've ever met, you'll end up believing it. As a result, you'll find yourself continuing where you would have previously given up. In short, your thoughts will crystallize into belief—a belief that will directly influence your behavior.

Once a belief has crystallized, it will generate corresponding thoughts. For example, let's say you believe that you aren't good enough. In this case, when you receive a compliment while out on a date, you may ignore it and assume the person who delivered the compliment is just being polite. When your boss compliments you at work, you may answer that anybody could have done it. Such thoughts will further feed the original belief that you aren't good enough.

Now, let's identify where your beliefs come from.

2. The origins of beliefs

Have you ever wondered how your beliefs were created in the first place?

The answer is simple. Your beliefs were formed through:

1. Your inner self-talk, and
2. Any input you received from the external world (and how you interpreted that input).

Let's look at these components for a moment.

a. Your inner self-talk

While thoughts have no power in and of themselves, if you entertain specific thoughts over and over, and for long enough, they begin to turn into beliefs. And the more you repeat these thoughts, the stronger the associated beliefs will become. For instance, telling yourself that you are stupid once is inconsequential, but repeating it thousands of times isn't.

The simple truth is this: what you keep telling yourself tends to become your reality over time. The conversation you have with yourself creates your "reality", whether this conversation is happening consciously or unconsciously. And to make it perfectly clear, your reality is what you believe about yourself and the world around you.

If you insist on telling yourself that everything you do sucks and that you're an idiot, this is how you will end up perceiving yourself. Such internal self-talk will lead you to sell yourself short and, eventually, to give up on your dreams. And to top of all that, it will lead you to feel terrible about yourself.

Please note that your self-talk will inevitably be affected by your environment. For example, if your parents or teachers repeatedly tell you that you will never amount to anything, you will integrate that so-called truth and begin telling yourself the same thing without even realizing it.

This leads us to the second factor influencing your beliefs.

b. Any input from the external world

A majority of your beliefs were shaped during your childhood and come from external influences, which could be your parents, family members, classmates, teachers or the media.

For example, if your parents struggled with money, you may have developed a scarcity mindset. If they criticized you, you may have felt as though whatever you did would never be good enough. And you may have continued to feel that way even after you left home and gained your independence.

To change your beliefs, you must:

- Change your self-talk, and
- Choose your environment more consciously.

Later in this book, we will discuss how you can modify your self-talk and use your environment to reprogram your mind. But for now, let's further define what we call "belief" by separating true belief from false belief.

3. True belief vs. false belief

True belief is that which is energized with strong conviction and genuine desire and sustained over a long period of time. Such belief transcends setbacks and disappointments, and it bypasses criticism or cynicism.

True belief exists when you:

- Know deep down that you can and, eventually, will figure things out,
- Remain convinced of that "truth" for months or years while letting go of self-doubt,
- Refuse to let your environment stand in the way of your goals, and

- Move through your day with a rock-solid sense of inner confidence.

However, true belief is not arrogance. It's not being the loudest person in the room, nor is it showing off. While some people may appear overly confident, it doesn't mean they have learned how to use the power of belief. Conversely, just because someone doesn't *look* confident doesn't mean they aren't using this superpower.

I invite you to cultivate true belief by reconnecting with your inner self and by maintaining faith no matter what. Practice staying in that positive mental space where everything seems possible. Then, keep moving toward your goals with confidence for as long as is needed to reach them.

* * *

Action step

Using your action guide, evaluate how well you've integrated true belief in your life.

4. The difference between belief and delusion

When I started my personal development journey, I envisioned myself inspiring the lives of thousands, if not millions, of people. But I couldn't help wondering whether my vision was coming from my ego or whether it was my "destiny" or something similar. Perhaps, I was nothing more than delusional.

To find out, I decided to trust my intuition and go for it. For the first few years I faced nothing but setback after setback. Traffic on my blog was abysmal, my books weren't selling, and I was losing money. But I kept believing. I kept applying the power of belief, using all the concepts you'll discover in this book:

- I told myself that if others could make a living writing self-help books, so could I. These individuals were no better, smarter or more motivated than me.

- I trusted that I was on the right path and doing the right thing, so I kept moving forward.
- I reminded myself that I had years to develop my business.
- I reminded myself that, if I kept moving forward, I would eventually figure things out.
- I developed the identity of a person who never gives up.
- I conditioned my mind daily, using affirmations, positive self-talk and visualization.
- I thought about all the reasons why my vision *had* to become reality and what it would bring to me and to people around me.
- I cultivated self-compassion. Every time I felt down, I would remind myself that everything was okay.

By using the power of belief, I was able to achieve some of my biggest dreams. As I'm writing this, I'm now a full-time writer and have complete control over my work schedule. I can travel wherever I want and whenever I want. But, more importantly, I'm absolutely convinced that I'm *not* delusional.

But this success only happened because I took action. I didn't just daydream. I visualized my goals with a strong sense of commitment and the firm determination to make them a reality. Then, I acted.

Therefore, if you feel driven to try something, take the first step. You never know where it will lead you. Don't underestimate what you can accomplish long term. In a few short years, you could find yourself in a completely different place, physically, mentally, financially and spiritually.

Now let's review some key characteristics of belief so that you develop a better sense of what it is and how you can use it to improve your life.

* * *

Action step

Using your action guide, write down one of your biggest goals or dreams, then answer the questions below:

- How delusional are you regarding this goal?
- If you keep doing what you're currently doing, how likely are you to achieve this goal (realistically)?
- What would you need to do to ensure you reach your goal or significantly increase your chances of doing so?

THE FIVE CHARACTERISTICS OF BELIEF

To make the most of the power of belief, you must understand its main characteristics. In this section, we'll review five of them. Understanding these characteristics will give you confidence in your ability to use belief to make astonishing changes in your life.

1. Belief is a skill

 As the physically weak man can make himself strong by careful and patient training, so the man of weak thoughts can make them strong by exercising himself in right thinking.

— JAMES ALLEN, WRITER

Almost everything you want in life can be attained by developing specific skills. With determination and hard work, you can learn to become an eloquent speaker, a seasoned chess player, an advanced meditator, or a skilled writer. And you can also learn to believe. No matter how low your confidence may be currently, you can boost it dramatically, using the exercises described in this book.

Personally, I wasn't born confident. For many years, I felt inadequate and insecure, wondering why I struggled so much to be assertive, confident or proactive. For instance, at school, I was too afraid to raise my hand and would often be unable to go to the bathroom (sometimes for hours). I wouldn't dare blow my nose either—or do anything else that would draw attention to myself. And when someone asked me for something, I wouldn't be able to say no. As years passed, my friends seemed to get ahead in life while I was unhappy at work and unsuccessful in my relationships. I continually asked myself why life was so unfair. After all, I worked hard and deserved better, right?

Perhaps, but I wasn't using the power of belief.

Now, let's be honest, I'm no Muhammad Ali or Bruce Lee. In some situations, I still feel inadequate, hesitant or embarrassed, but in the past few years I've made tremendous progress. Reading countless self-help books has allowed me to grasp the power of belief and use it to develop the level of confidence needed to achieve many of my goals. I realized that, by cultivating unshakeable belief, almost anything I envisioned and genuinely desired was possible. The only job left to do was to "purify" my mind by:

1. Eliminating self-doubt, and
2. Replacing it with thoughts of confidence, courage and certainty.

Once equipped with this absolute confidence, I could go on to explore new horizons, new possibilities and discover the hidden talents I didn't even know I had. One way I developed higher levels of self-belief was by achieving small goals consistently and repeatedly. Concretely, I did this by:

- Learning to keep the promises I made to myself (by achieving small goals at first and bigger ones later one), and by
- Learning to keep promises to others (by honoring my promises wherever and whenever possible).

Over time, I attained bigger and bigger goals. Having developed so much confidence, I now know I can reach most of the goals I set.

The take home lesson is this:

- You must realize that your ability to keep your word is key to cultivate strong self-belief, and
- You can start today by setting small goals and achieving them consistently.

Remember, belief is a skill that you have access to and can develop the same way as anybody else. When you follow the right process, you can move from a state of perpetual self-doubt to one of extreme self-belief. So why not start practicing this skill so you can create the life you want in the coming years?

In **PART IV.** *The Belief Formula*, we'll explore a specific formula you can use to develop rock-solid confidence.

* * *

Action step

Answer the questions below using your action guide:

- What are you currently doing to develop greater belief in yourself and in your vision?
- What could you be doing to cultivate even more belief in yourself?

2. Belief is neutral

 Nature is neutral. Nature doesn't care. If you do what other successful people do, you will enjoy the same results and rewards that they do. And if you don't, you won't.

— BRIAN TRACY, AUTHOR AND MOTIVATIONAL SPEAKER.

Another fundamental aspect of belief is that it is neutral. Nature is impartial and couldn't care less who develops unshakeable self-confidence and who doesn't. As such, nature cannot prevent anyone from using the power of belief to improve their life. This goes even for people experiencing intense guilt, crippling self-doubt or any other life challenges. It's worth repeating:

Nature cannot stop you from using your ability to believe to accomplish incredible deeds and transform your life beyond imagination.

All you have to do is decide on the level of belief you want to acquire over time. Do you want to develop extraordinary belief so that you can grow and create countless new opportunities for yourself, or do you want to play it small, doubting every step along the way? The choice is yours, but so are the consequences you'll have to live with.

The bottom line is, belief is neutral. The act of believing is a tool available to all of us. Use it to design your ideal life and uncover your potential—or don't. Either way, the universe doesn't care.

Action step

Answer the following questions using your action guide:

- Knowing that nobody can prevent you from believing, how will you use your power of belief starting today?

- What will you use it for?

3. Belief is your responsibility

   ❝ You cannot escape the responsibility of tomorrow by evading it today.

— ABRAHAM LINCOLN, FORMER PRESIDENT OF THE UNITED
STATES.

Wouldn't it be nice if you had a supportive family, encouraging friends, knowledgeable mentors and world-class coaches around you 24/7?

Sadly, for most of us, it's not the case. Your family might ridicule your dreams, your friends may be unsupportive and you may not have any mentors or coaches to guide you. But that's okay. You don't need anyone's permission to use the power of belief. Believing is inherent to your nature. Nobody can ever take that ability away from you. Therefore, it's your responsibility to use your innate belief to design the life you want. Should you choose to take it, your job is to find a way to develop unshakeable confidence regardless of your environment. So, don't use your environment as an excuse to ignore your inner power of belief. That would be selling yourself short. Instead, reclaim and utilize your ability to believe. It's your responsibility to do so.

* * *

Action steps

Complete the exercises below using your action guide:

- For a moment, close your eyes and let the following truth sink in: you can and will cultivate rock-solid belief over time. Accept this fact as undeniable.

- Now, knowing belief is your responsibility, write down one thing you will do to regain control over your power of belief (e.g., by joining a group of like-minded people, distancing yourself from a toxic person or reading biographies from successful people).

4. Belief is ever-present

 Man is made by his belief. As he believes, so he is.

— JOHANN WOLFGANG VON GOETHE, POET.

Another fundamental characteristic of belief is that it is always present. Your inner ability to believe can *never* be taken away from you. It can only be forgotten or temporarily covered with self-doubt. This means you have within yourself the ability to wake every day and believe one more time, regardless of yesterday's apparent failures. Only the idea you can lose that power may cause you to doubt yourself. Of course, we all doubt ourselves from time to time, but keep in mind that, after moments of self-doubt, you can always choose to refocus on your power to believe. Furthermore, if you doubt yourself more often than you'd like too, make sure you apply the technique introduced in **Part IV**. *The Belief Formula* to boost your level of self-belief.

Belief is available at all times. So, tap into your power as often as necessary and begin to accomplish your wildest goals.

* * *

Action steps

Complete the following exercises using your action guide:

- Take a moment to notice the fact that your ability to believe can never be taken from you. Realize that, at this very moment, you can *choose* to believe.

- Then, write down what you would do differently if you were absolutely convinced that the power of belief was with you at all times.

5. Belief is a gift you give to the world

66 It is not my place to judge any person's beliefs, but choose rather to celebrate their ability to believe.

— TOM ALTHOUSE, ACTOR AND WRITER.

As you start pursuing your goals with greater self-confidence, you might fear being rejected, sounding arrogant or being seen as selfish. However, bear in mind that the power of belief should not be used for selfish motives (although it could be). It should be used to transform yourself and, perhaps more importantly, to transform the world around you in a positive way.

I invite you to see belief as a gift you give not only to yourself but also to the world. By using this gift, you can plant the seeds of possibility inside yourself and inside the minds of people who cross your path. As you do so, you become a source of inspiration for the people around you.

In truth, each of us has a role to play by offering the gift of belief to people who need it the most. We might not be the next Gandhi or Mother Theresa, but by the way we behave and interact with others, we may create the spark needed to awaken the untapped potential in others. This alone is a true blessing and a humbling realization.

Therefore, rather than letting self-doubt dictate your life, why not use your new understanding of belief to inspire your spouse, kids, friends, colleagues and everyone you encounter in your life? Why not become a beacon of hope and positivity for others? While belief might be intangible, it can have tangible effects on the world. Use your belief to influence people and create a positive ripple effect all around you.

* * *

Action step

Answer the following questions using your action guide:

- If you dramatically increased your level of self-belief, who around you would be impacted positively?
- Who would be inspired?

3

THE POWER OF BELIEF

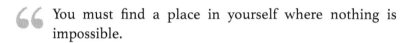 You must find a place in yourself where nothing is impossible.

— Deepak Chopra, author and public speaker.

Belief is one of the most powerful forces on earth. Once you learn how to use it properly, you can make astonishing changes in your life. Let's see in more detail how belief creates your reality.

1. Belief distorts reality

The ability to believe is your superpower. The power of belief can enable you to bend reality to your will—at least, that's how it may feel to you. Belief can "distort" reality by:

1. Changing how you think, feel and act, opening doors to countless opportunities that didn't exist before,
2. Turning your subconscious into a powerful ally,
3. Influencing people around you, and
4. Inspiring people.

Let's go over these four points in more depth.

a. Belief changes the way you think, feel and act

Adopting empowering beliefs impacts the way you think, which triggers new feelings and leads you to take different actions. In turn, these actions enable you to achieve better results. In short, belief allows you to distort your "reality" by introducing new ways of thinking that enhance your field of possibilities.

For instance, if you believe you can always become better at everything you do, you'll look for ways to improve. You can do this by asking for feedback, tweaking your approach, finding a mentor or just by trying one more time. Since your new identity dictates that improvement is inevitable, you will keep going until reality "bends to your will". On the other hand, if you don't believe improvement is possible for you, you will not make any effort, or at least not enough effort to see tangible results. This, in turn, will reinforce the idea that you are powerless.

b. Belief turns your subconscious into a powerful ally

Another side effect of having empowering beliefs is that your subconscious will start working for you. When you have strong convictions, your subconscious will strive to close the gap between your current situation and what you want to become true.

For example, if you're convinced you can design a fulfilling career, your subconscious will look for opportunities to make that belief come true. As a result, you might bump into someone who loves his or her job and receive invaluable advice from them. You might watch a YouTube video that will put you on the right track. Or you might suddenly develop ingenious solutions to help you create your ideal career.

In other words, when you believe something is possible, your subconscious will begin to close the gap between where you are and where you want to be. It will identify valuable information you might otherwise have missed. This is why I invite you to gain clarity regarding what you want and ask your subconscious to support your endeavors.

c. Belief influences people around you

Another reason belief is so important is because it influences your environment. You can use the power of belief not only to impact your thoughts, feelings and actions, but also to influence every single person you meet.

The famous life coach, Tony Robbins, says that in any interaction between two people, the person with the most certainty wins. And it is indeed easier to sell anything—whether it is yourself, a business idea or a product you have created—when you have absolute belief in what you're selling.

Beliefs act as pillars. When these pillars are strong, no external events can shatter them. You can listen to people but remain unaffected by their judgments. You may encounter failures or crises but keep believing in yourself. Regardless of your external environment, you will stay inside your bubble of confidence, protected from the negativity around you.

When you navigate through the world with such a strong sense of belief, you will continually think, feel and act according to your core beliefs. As you do so, you will be far more likely to influence people around you than the other way around. This is because you use the power of belief while others don't.

In **PART III.** *Building fundamental beliefs*, we'll introduce core beliefs you can adopt to build your confidence and begin to influence people rather than being influenced by them.

d. Belief inspires people

As you apply the power of belief, you'll find yourself in a better position to inspire the people around you. You'll understand that no matter what their narrative may be, they also have the ability to believe, figure things out and achieve most of their goals. You'll stop seeing people for who they currently are. Instead, you'll see them for who they *could become* once they remove their mental blocks and their self-imposed limitations. As I said previously, this is why belief is a gift you give both to yourself and to the people around you. By using its power, you can grow and provide a positive impact the world around you at a far greater scale than you otherwise would.

Many successful people can see others for who they could become. This is because successful individuals understand how belief works and how it can magnify other people's abilities. On the other hand, people who struggle with self-doubt are unable to see potential in others. Since these people don't believe they can grow, they don't believe others can grow either.

As you learn to use the power of belief, you'll become a source of inspiration for people around you. In your presence, many people will be inspired to challenge themselves and overcome their perceived limitations.

* * *

Action step

Think of one of the most empowering beliefs you could adopt. Then answer the questions below:

- How can my subconscious help me make this belief come true (e.g., could it help me develop solutions, lead me to take different actions, et cetera)?
- How will my new belief affect the people around me?
- If I am able to see more potential in people than they see in themselves, in what way will I become an inspiration to them? How will I support them?

2. Your thoughts create your reality

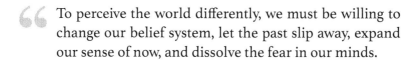 To perceive the world differently, we must be willing to change our belief system, let the past slip away, expand our sense of now, and dissolve the fear in our minds.

People often misunderstand the idea that "thoughts create reality". They fail to realize there is always a gap between the time they think of something and the moment it starts manifesting in the real world. It's not as though they can have a thought and voilà, what they envision immediately appears. This would be impractical for many reasons.

We have thousands of thoughts every day including many toxic ones. Imagine what would happen if these thoughts were all to manifest instantly. The world would be in a complete state of chaos. How would you feel if I held you accountable for insulting your boss or hitting one of your colleagues in the face just because you thought of doing it?

Fortunately, reality doesn't work this way. Your thoughts have the power to become reality only when sustained over a long enough period of time and charged with a strong enough mental energy—the energy of belief, conviction and commitment.

A thought obeying this rule will lead you to start acting accordingly and, over time, will generate the desired results. Of course, there are limits to what is possible in this world, but these limits are usually lower than the ones you impose on yourself. Therefore, the first step to turning your thoughts into reality is to believe that whatever you envision is possible. Sure, you might not reach it, but you can at least make tremendous progress toward it—often beyond your imagination.

Below are specific examples of how thoughts actually work.

Imagine you want to travel to South East Asia with your family. First, you might have the thought, "One day, I'd love to travel to South East Asia with my family". Now, is this enough to make your wish come true? Of course not.

First, the thought must be energized. It must be accompanied by excitement and desire. Without desire, a thought has no power. You must feel as though your thoughts are pulling you. They must put you in a different mental state and teleport you into the future you want to live in. In this example, you must truly *desire* to travel to South East Asia and already see yourself there.

Second, you must further energize it through commitment. That is, in your mind, you must commit to turning that thought into reality. Many people like to daydream about a better future. However, you cannot transform your life this way. Daydreaming makes you feel good in the moment, while at the same time, knowing that your dreams will most likely never happen. On the other hand, *committing* is stepping into your future and firmly believing it will become your reality. These are two opposing mental attitudes. In our example, you must be absolutely determined to travel to South East Asia with your family.

Third, you must revisit the same thought as many times as necessary until it generates the impulse to act. Just having a thought once won't have much impact. However, when you think the same thought many times throughout your day, you'll feel compelled to act to close the gap between your current situation and the desired one. In this instance you must think of your travel to South East Asia and visualize it as vividly as possible until it becomes an important enough goal to be acted upon.

Remember, the power of belief is what allows us to turn something intangible (a thought, idea or vision) into something tangible (an item, company, travel experience, et cetera). For instance, this book started with the following thought:

Belief is one of the most powerful forces on earth. I want to help people use it so that they can change their lives and the lives of the people around them.

Then, I kept directing my mental energy toward this thought until I felt compelled to put words on paper and create this book. Similarly:

- When given enough intensity, the thought, "I want to change career" leads us to learn new skills, apply for job interviews or network until we successfully switch career.

- When given enough attention, the thought, "I want to retire early" entices us to save more money and/or start side hustles until we reach that goal.
- When given enough importance, the thought, "I want to find a partner" drives us to start using dating apps and socializing more often until we find someone we want to be with.

In 2017, I quit my well-paid job to become a full-time writer. Many people must have thought I was crazy. Yet, I had little doubt I would make it as a writer.

Why?

Mostly, because I already understood how I could use the power of belief to close the gap between my present situation and the future I envisioned. At the time, I had also:

- Already written five books,
- Received many positive reviews for my books,
- Worked hard on my side business while having a full-time job (which proved I was motivated), and
- Completed enough personal development work to understand that only a lack of belief could prevent me from achieving my goals.

In short, I had developed the confidence needed, and the belief required, to design the future I had in mind.

To conclude, in many cases, your thoughts create your reality. So, make sure you use the power of belief to close the gap between where you are and where you want to be.

To learn in greater depth about the thinking process that allowed me to become a full-time writer, you can refer to *Master Your Thinking*, the fifth book in this series.

* * *

Action step

Complete the following exercise using the action guide:

- Think of one thing you want to see happening in the future, for example getting a promotion, finding a better job or traveling overseas.
- Imagine if that one thing became your single point of focus.
- Then write down in your action guide what specific actions you will start taking as a result of focusing on that thought.

3. Your belief determines your results

 If you believe you can, you probably can. If you believe you won't, you most assuredly won't. Belief is the ignition switch that gets you off the launching pad.

— Denis Waitley, motivational speaker and writer.

a. Life is a simulation game

I like to compare life to a simulation game. In this game, the major component that determines your results is:

Your level of self-belief.

You can use the power of your mind to boost your self-belief. Your mind acts like the main controller of the game. It determines whether you'll play it small (and stay at level 1) or give it all (and aim for level 100). Once you learn to discipline your mind and maintain a high level of confidence, you'll find yourself accomplishing wonderful things.

On the other hand, if you fall victim to self-doubt, you'll achieve far less than you're capable of achieving. Self-doubt consumes your energy, weakens your thoughts and diminishes your creative power. Self-doubt destroys your ability to focus on a single thought strongly enough and for long enough to accumulate the energy required for the manifestation of its physical equivalent. So, eliminate needless worries and remove any limitations standing between you and your goals. Then, concentrate your thoughts on what you desire the most. To learn how to identify your limitations and begin to overcome them, refer to **PART II.** *Identifying your limiting beliefs.*

Once I understood that gaining control over my mind was the secret to achieving almost anything I desired, I committed to developing rock-solid confidence. In other words, I chose to move away from level 1 (crippling self-doubt) and work my way toward level 100 (unshakeable belief).

What about you? At what level do you want to play the game called, "your life"? Starting today, what do you need to do differently to reach that level?

Remember, your level of belief largely determines what you can accomplish in this world. Starting today, choose at what level you want to play the game and act accordingly.

* * *

Action step

Using your action guide, answer the questions below:

- If I were to rate my current level of self-belief on a scale from 1 (playing it small) to 100 (giving it all), what would it be?
- What do I want my level of self-belief to be thirty days from now?
- What can I do to get there?

b. Belief makes the impossible possible

You may have been told to be realistic, but have you ever considered what being realistic actually means? This concept is subjective. For instance, what *you* believe you can do and what *I* believe I can do may vary significantly. These variations largely depend on our individual levels of self-belief, our unique experiences, and our specific skills, along with other factors.

My advice is: don't let other people tell you what you can or cannot do. Their opinion is irrelevant. If I had waited for other people's stamp of approval to start writing, I would still be waiting. When I started my career, I had no writing degree, I didn't know anyone in the industry, and I wasn't even writing in my mother tongue. Yet, from my own perspective, my goal was realistic. So, I ignored the negative opinions and criticisms and began my journey.

I invite you to do the same. Stop waiting for other people's approval to pursue your goals. You don't need their permission to start living the life you want. Forget about other people's definitions of "realistic". Instead, use the power of belief to make the seemingly impossible, possible. If you can be "crazy" enough to believe your dreams are possible—and remain in that mental state for long enough—you will get there. As Henry Ford said, "Whether you think you can or you can't, either way you're right." You will only start taking the actions needed to reach your goals when you truly *believe* you can achieve them.

* * *

Action steps

Complete the following exercises using your action guide:

- For a moment, forget about all the limitations other people may be imposing on you. Instead, focus on what the absolute best version of yourself could accomplish.
- Now, ask yourself, "What 'impossible' things can I make possible in the near future?"

c. The size of your thinking determines the size of your accomplishments

Your dominant thoughts are a good predictor of your future. For instance, if your daily thoughts are dominated by what you'll have for dinner, what you'll watch on Netflix tonight or what new gadget you'll buy, you're unlikely to perform at your absolute best or achieve your biggest dreams. On the other hand, if you keep focusing on major goals, you will force yourself to think bigger and become better in order to reach them.

Whenever you look at visionaries, you'll notice they think at a completely different level from the norm. For example, they may ask themselves questions such as:

- What does the absolute best version of myself look like?
- What is the biggest impact I can have on the world?
- How can I become a world-class expert in my field?
- How can I accelerate my results exponentially?
- What skills do I need to learn and who do I need to meet to make my vision a reality?
- How can I revolutionize my industry?
- And so on.

When asked repeatedly over a long enough period of time, such questions will lead to better results than trivial questions such as, what to eat for dinner or what movie to watch on Netflix. Remember, to use the power of belief you must entertain the same thoughts repeatedly while putting mental effort and a sense of commitment into it.

So, what are your dominant thoughts right now? Do they match the future you want to create, or are they too small? Starting today, what better thoughts could you adopt?

* * *

Action step

Answer the questions below using your action guide:

- These days, what do I think about most often? What are my dominant thoughts?
- If I keep having these same thoughts, what's likely to happen in the future?
- Is this what I really want? If not, what dominant thoughts should I adopt instead?

4. Confidence vs. arrogance

 We ask ourselves, 'Who am I to be brilliant, gorgeous, talented, fabulous?' Actually, who are you not to be?

— MARIANNE WILLIAMSON, AUTHOR AND POLITICIAN.

Bruce Lee used the power of belief to cultivate unshakeable confidence. In January 1969, 28-year-old Bruce Lee was a minor TV star in the United States. He was a father of two and had little financial security. At this time, he wrote the following mission statement:

SECRET

My Definite Chief Aim

I, Bruce Lee, will be the first highest paid Oriental super star in the United States. In return I will give the most exciting performances and render the best of quality in the capacity of an actor. Starting in 1970, I will achieve world fame and from then onward till the end of 1980 I will have in my possession $10,000,000. I will live the way I please and achieve inner harmony and happiness.

Bruce Lee

Jan. 1969

In his own words, this unshakeable confidence went beyond even faith:

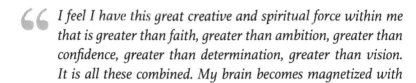

> *I feel I have this great creative and spiritual force within me that is greater than faith, greater than ambition, greater than confidence, greater than determination, greater than vision. It is all these combined. My brain becomes magnetized with this domination force which I hold in my hand.*

Similarly, the boxer, Muhammad Ali, said, *"I'm a the greatest, I said that even before I knew I was."* By broadcasting to the world who he was (or wanted to be), he started creating his own reality.

Of course, this kind of self-talk doesn't automatically turn someone into the greatest boxer or martial artist in the world, but it is the foundation. This belief must then be backed up with consistent hard work sustained over a long period of time.

Now, when someone states they're the greatest boxer of all time or the "highest paid Oriental super star in the United States", is it delusion? Is it arrogance or is it the unshakeable self-belief used to "predict" the future? This is hard to say, but I believe you, too, must risk being seen as arrogant as you practice developing unshakeable belief. Nothing is wrong with building rock-solid confidence. In fact, by using the power of belief, you can transform lives, empower people and turn desperate situations into hopeful ones. And, of course, you can also achieve most of your goals.

I sometimes worry that people around me may think I'm bragging. However, sharing my stories and goals is a way to hold myself accountable and demand more of myself—and hopefully to inspire my readers to reach their own goals. I've decided that building the confidence needed to reach my goals was more important than the negative opinion of others.

So, learn to assert yourself. Affirm your long-term goals. Broadcast to the world who you are becoming. And begin to turn the invisible—your dreams, ideals and vision—into the visible. You have the power to believe. Use it to achieve your most exciting goals.

Now, let's see what you can do to identify your limiting beliefs and start overcoming them.

PART II

IDENTIFYING YOUR LIMITING BELIEFS

The man who knows his limitations, has none.

— DAVID FOSTER WALLACE, AUTHOR.

No matter how successful we may be, we still have limiting beliefs holding us back. I believe that one of our goals in life should be to learn to let go of our limitations so that we can be true to ourselves and achieve all the things we genuinely want.

Imagine if you could eradicate all your limitations and develop an absolute confidence in your ability to achieve any goal you set. How would that make you feel? How much more energy, enthusiasm and passion would you have?

In this section, we'll work on uncovering some of your most limiting beliefs and see how you can replace them with more empowering ones so you can start unlocking your potential.

But, before we do that, let's see how your beliefs shape your current identity and, more importantly, what all the implications are.

4

BELIEF AND IDENTITY

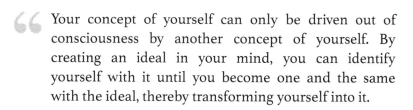 Your concept of yourself can only be driven out of consciousness by another concept of yourself. By creating an ideal in your mind, you can identify yourself with it until you become one and the same with the ideal, thereby transforming yourself into it.

— NEVILLE GODDARD, AUTHOR, *THE POWER OF AWARENESS.*

Whatever you believe shapes your identity. To grow and overcome your current limitations, you must reinvent yourself and change your identity. For instance, to move from a struggling writer to a successful one, I had to change my identity. I had to see myself for who I could become, not for who I was at the time. I had to believe that if others could become successful writers, I could too. It took me several years before I could actually see myself as a "real" writer and introduce myself as such. When asked what I was doing, I would usually say something such as:

"I'm writing short books and selling them on Amazon."

Does that make me sound like a real writer to you?

However, then I decided to create a new identity. I chose to embody the writer I aspired to be and began to introduce myself accordingly. I wasn't writing short books, no. I was now running an online publishing business. I was both a professional writer and a businessman. From that point onward, I made sure I used the words "online publishing business", and "writer" every time I introduced myself.

At the time, I dreamt of becoming a six-figure author. So, the next step was to behave like one. Whenever I hesitated to invest in books or courses, I asked myself the following question: "If I truly want to become a six-figure author, can I afford not to invest in this product?" I also read numerous stories, blog posts and books from successful self-published authors. By absorbing their way of thinking, scrutinizing their behavior and learning from their experience, I intended to maximize my chances of success.

Similarly, your limiting beliefs can make you feel less capable than you really are. They may lead you to feel unworthy or incapable of achieving certain goals. But whatever identity you're currently hanging onto is not you—it is merely a concept you've *accepted* as true.

Fortunately, you can change many of your beliefs and create a new identity. You can see yourself as a top performer, a charismatic leader or a confident businessperson. You can envision yourself being world-class at any endeavor you choose to pursue.

Now, let me show you how your identity shapes your behavior. The example below is taken from my book, *Success is Inevitable*.

Imagine you're currently fifty pounds overweight and have been struggling to lose weight for years. Now, put yourself in the shoes of a personal trainer with the "ideal weight". Imagine you—the personal trainer—woke up one day carrying an extra fifty pounds of unwanted weight. How would you react?

I'm betting you would be shocked. You would think, "This is not who I am!" and would instantly start transforming your body. To do so, you would remove all junk food from your house and keep exercising until you returned to your ideal weight. And you would succeed. Why? Because you have a specific image of what your body should look like, and this image is so closely linked to your identity, you would inevitably return to your original weight.

What this example demonstrates is that people act according to their beliefs. And these beliefs are the results of the identity they've created for themselves either consciously or unconsciously. Therefore, to change how they act, people need to adopt new beliefs and create a new identity.

Below is another example of how our beliefs dictate our choices and shape our destiny. This is taken from Jack Canfield's book, *Success Principles*.

Victor Serebriakoff, the son of a Russian émigré, grew up in a London slum. His teachers didn't believe he could finish school, so they convinced him to find a job instead. As a result, he dropped out of education when he was fifteen and moved from one dead-end job to the next.

However, one event transformed his life. When aged thirty-two, he joined the British army and was given an intelligence test. The test revealed he had an IQ of 161. In short, he was incredibly smart.

Upon seeing the results, he immediately started acting like a genius. After leaving the army he worked for a timber company and eventually become the manager of several factories. Even more impressive, he invented a machine for grading timber and introduced the metric system to the trade, which profoundly impacted the industry. Later, he became the chairman of a national timber standards commission.

The lesson here is that, while Victor had *always been* smart, he let people tell him otherwise. He believed them and acted accordingly for over fifteen years. By doing so, he allowed his (perceived) limitations to dictate his identity and shape his destiny.

These are two vivid illustrations of how limiting beliefs can negatively affect our lives.

What about you? Are you letting your current perceived limitations determine your identity and, thus, your future?

* * *

Action step

Complete the exercises below using your action guide:

* Think of one major goal you'd like to achieve.
* Now, write down a few statements that would describe the identity of someone who has already achieved that goal.

Choosing your identity

Now, you might wonder how you can change your identity. Well, in a sense, it is simple. It starts with a choice. It begins with a decision to embody certain character traits and to behave consistently in a way that aligns with those traits.

After I graduated from business school in 2015, I joined a small consulting firm. Twice a year, we had to deliver a presentation as part of our evaluation. We were given a project and had to create a proposal we would present to the company asking for our help (our supervisors would play that role). I tried to come up with a decent proposal, but as I was unable to produce anything remotely good, I received the worse grades in the entire company—twice in a row. It made me ashamed, especially considering the majority of my peers were fresh graduates almost ten years younger than me. Shortly after, I quit my job to focus on my writing career.

After leaving my job, I made a deliberate choice to change my identity. I didn't want to be average anymore. From that point on, I would be world-class. I would become excellent. So, I asked myself, "What do high performers do, and how can I become one?" I realized that one common point shared by high performers is when they say something, they do it. In short, they deliver on what they promise, both to themselves and to others. Therefore, to join the rank, I would have to develop that ability. For me, it entailed becoming the most disciplined person I knew. One way I built my new identity was by setting small goals and achieving them consistently. Doing so instilled in me the confidence to achieve bigger and bigger goals. In addition, I cultivated the habit of only saying yes to the things I could deliver on. I wanted to keep my promises as much as humanly possible. By implementing these habits alongside a few others, I was able to raise my standards and obtain better results.

Remember, most of your limitations are self-imposed. They are false identities you accept as true. By using the power of belief, you can design a new identity that will enable you to accomplish almost anything you desire.

The bottom line is, your beliefs impact your behaviors and largely determine your results. So, choose them carefully. In **PART III.** *Building fundamental beliefs*, we'll go over some of the core beliefs that will enable you to boost your confidence and enhance your results.

Now that we've seen how your beliefs affect your identity and determine many of your life choices, let's see how to identify your limiting beliefs and overcome them.

OVERCOMING YOUR LIMITING BELIEFS

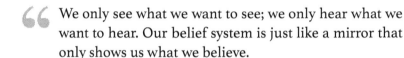 We only see what we want to see; we only hear what we want to hear. Our belief system is just like a mirror that only shows us what we believe.

— DON MIGUEL RUIZ, SPIRITUAL TEACHER AND AUTHOR.

1. Identifying your limiting beliefs

Imagine if you could eliminate any self-imposed limitations and irrational fears. How much more confident would you become, and how much more would you accomplish as a result?

The truth is, most of the things holding you back are excuses. These excuses are preventing you from improving your life. They mostly hold power because you accept them as true or as valid in your situation. But is that so? Is there *really* nothing you can do about these limitations? Are you *really* that powerless?

To identify your limiting beliefs, you can ask yourself the following questions for each area of your life:

- How come I'm not at a ten out of ten in this area?

- What's holding me back?
- If I couldn't make any excuses, what would I do differently?

Bear in mind that any excuse you make reduces your field of possibilities. By tolerating excuses, you give your power away to external circumstances. You say to the world, "It's not in my power. There is nothing I can do about it."

However, in truth, you can almost always do something to improve your life. Even if you can't change your situation, you can change your perception of it.

I had many valid reasons not to write self-help books. Millions of people probably had more legitimacy to write on that topic. Some of my reasons were:

- I have no writing degree,
- I have no degree in psychology, coaching or any personal development related topic,
- I'm introverted and not the type of person you would imagine as a personal development "guru",
- I don't know anyone in the industry,
- I write in English but I'm not a native speaker,
- The personal development niche is highly competitive, and
- Many people don't believe I will make it.

So of course I had self-doubt. Who was I to write a book? Everything has already been said anyway. And why me when so many others are more qualified?

The problem when we accept such excuses is that they tend to become our reality. Unless we replace them with more empowering beliefs, we risk selling ourselves short. To let go of our excuses, we must choose to adopt new thoughts that support the reality we want to create.

An example of a limiting belief I often give is:

I don't have enough time.

Now, we can replace this belief with a more empowering one such as:

I always make the time to do whatever I'm committed to achieving.

In truth, even the most successful people on the planet can manage to find the time to exercise, read or travel with their family. If Barack Obama found the time to exercise every day when he was at the White House, don't you think you can, too?

As you repeatedly tell yourself that you make the time to work on whatever you're committed to, you'll find yourself thinking and acting differently. You'll ask yourself, "How do I find the time?" In the process, you'll discover you can create more time. Perhaps you can:

- Cut down the time you spend watching TV,
- Stop wasting thirty minutes a day scrolling your Facebook newsfeed,
- Cook several meals at once,
- Delegate some of your chores, or
- Say no to requests that aren't aligned with your values or vision.

As you can see, you have more control over your time and your life than you think.

The bottom line is, you can always come up with excuses for not working. However, what separates people with high self-belief from others is that they continually look for reasons they will succeed— not reasons they will fail. Having mastered the power of belief, they find themselves achieving one goal after the other.

What about you? What are your excuses, and what are you going to do about them?

* * *

Action step

Using your action guide, complete the exercise below:

- Select the one area of your life you most want to focus on right now. Consider the following areas: career, family, finance, personal growth, relationships, social life, spirituality. Then, answer the question below.
- How come I'm not at a ten out of ten in this area?
- Write down two to three excuses you could remove/work on that would have the biggest positive impact in your life.

Now, let's see how you can start letting go of these excuses by choosing a new identity that better serves you and your plans.

2. Challenging your limiting beliefs

Once you have identified some of your limiting beliefs, you need to challenge them. To do so, start by asking yourself the following question:

Are my limiting beliefs always true all the time in every circumstance?

Limiting beliefs are usually false, at least partially. For instance, the belief you're not a confident person is probably widely inaccurate. You may lack confidence in specific situations but may be confident in others. The same goes for the previous example, "I don't have enough time". Fundamentally speaking, you're not a person who lacks time. There may be periods when you're busy and others when you are less so. You probably have busy and less busy days. Nonetheless, you always have room to choose what to prioritize.

3. Finding counterexamples in your life

An effective way to challenge your limiting beliefs is to look at counterexamples in your personal life, i.e., examples that clearly show your beliefs aren't as true as you think they are.

Let's say you believe you aren't good enough which leads you to feel inadequate and ashamed of yourself. Now are you really not good enough all the time in every circumstance, or is this true only in specific circumstances?

The likelihood is you feel more confident in certain situations than in others, but do you acknowledge these situations? The main difference between people with healthy self-esteem and people with low self-esteem is in what they focus on. The former acknowledges all the things they're doing well. The latter blame themselves for every little thing they do wrong, while failing to acknowledge their accomplishments.

As you proactively look for things you do or did well, you'll find plenty of examples. Then, you'll realize your "I'm not good enough" belief, doesn't hold true anymore, or at least you'll begin to see how inaccurate it is.

The point is, you should gather specific examples that demonstrate your belief is, if not completely, at least partially inaccurate. Remember, many of the beliefs you hold about yourself and the world are false. They are part of the story you're telling yourself, and this story can be changed to serve you better.

So, challenge your beliefs and see them for what they are—beliefs— and not accurate pictures of reality.

* * *

Action steps

Using your action guide, complete the following exercise:

- Select one limiting belief and answer the following question: Is this limiting belief always true all the time in any circumstance?
- Then look for examples in your own life that show your limiting belief is inaccurate.

4. Gathering proof that your beliefs are inaccurate

To challenge your limiting beliefs further, look for case studies that directly contradict those beliefs. Sometimes, all you need is one example of someone succeeding at what you want to do. This can be enough to make you realize that, if one person can succeed, you can too.

For example, you may hold the belief rich people are greedy. If so, it's unlikely you'll make the amount of money you desire. After all, you wouldn't want to be associated with greedy people, would you?

However, as you look around, you'll find that many wealthy people care about others and spend their money generously. Now, can rich people be greedy? Of course, but so can less fortunate people. Money simply makes people's greediness seem more apparent to others.

So, if you want to let go of such disempowering beliefs, look for wealthy people with whom you can identify for their kindness and generosity.

Or perhaps you believe you're not smart enough and, therefore, can't build that exciting business you've been dreaming about. Nor can you earn more money from doing so. But is this true?

A short while ago, I learned a friend of a friend was running his own business very successfully. I have to admit I was a little shocked. This specific person didn't appear particularly brilliant to me. Yet, there he was, running his own business. This example shows you don't need to be special to make money, you simply need to understand how money works, develop a healthy relationship with it, and, more importantly, believe in yourself for long enough until you achieve your goals.

You may also believe you don't have enough time to work on your side business. If so, look for people who've created a successful side business despite having an insanely busy schedule. In a Facebook group for writers, I read a post from a woman who wrote twenty-six novels in one year while having two kids and holding down a full-time job as a high-school teacher. Furthermore, she was a very successful writer, earning a great living.

As you gather relevant case studies like this one, you'll begin to see that what you thought impossible might not be. After all, if others can succeed, why not you? The belief that "If others can, I can", helped me move from an aspiring writer to a successful one. And I'm not the only one who's benefiting from it. Maria, one of my readers, learned seven languages in seven years without spending any money. Guess what one of the beliefs she relied on to reach that goal was? Yes, you're right, "If others can, I can".

So, look for relevant case studies. Then, remember that if others can, you probably can too.

* * *

Action step

Look at the limiting belief you identified in the previous exercise. Now, gather case studies to demonstrate why this belief is inaccurate. Then, write them down in your action guide.

6

INTEGRATING YOUR NEW BELIEFS

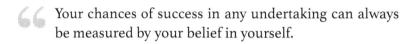 Your chances of success in any undertaking can always be measured by your belief in yourself.

— ROBERT COLLIER, AUTHOR.

Finally, you want to integrate your new beliefs to make them part of your identity. You can do this by:

1. Writing them down and looking at them on a regular basis,
2. Thinking about them often,
3. Acting in a way that strengthens them,
4. Thinking of all the reasons why they are accurate, and
5. Thinking of all the reasons why you want them to be true.

1. Write down your empowering beliefs

The first thing I invite you to do is to write your beliefs down. The simple act of writing things down can be beneficial in two ways. First, it forces you to process your thoughts and put them on paper in a clear and articulate way. This alone brings clarity. Second, it makes them more real to you. When you write things down, it's as though you are turning something intangible, like a thought, into something more real, like a specific intention, a clear goal, et cetera.

Therefore, write down the empowering beliefs you want to replace your limiting beliefs with. When you do so, make sure you:

- State your beliefs in the present tense,
- Avoid using negatives and state your beliefs in the positive form (e.g., say "I'm courageous" rather than "I'm no longer afraid"),
- Add power to your affirmation by changing your physiological state (e.g., engage your body and experiment with different vocal tones), and
- Use the power of visualization and see yourself in specific situations that relate to your belief, then try to feel as though you already have what you want (see the section *Using the power of visualization*).

Some examples of empowering beliefs are:

- I make the time to do whatever I'm committed to,
- If others can, I can,
- I'm the most persistent person I know,
- I'm worthy of love, and
- I'm as capable as anyone else.

2. Think about your empowering beliefs often

The next step is to think about your empowering beliefs repeatedly until they become part of your identity. For example, a good idea is to put your beliefs on paper and display that piece of paper somewhere you can see it every day, whether it be on your wall, work desk or bedside table.

3. Act according to your beliefs

Behave according to your beliefs as often as possible. For instance, to strengthen the belief "I find the time to do whatever I'm committed to", make sure you release time to work on things that matter to you. Of course, thinking of your belief often will also help you act accordingly by creating a positive feedback loop.

Remember, you're creating a new identity here, so think of all the ways someone embodying that identity would behave. If your new identity is "I'm a healthy person", ask yourself what a healthy person actually does. For instance, a healthy person might:

- Walk every day instead of taking the bus,
- Take the stairs instead of the elevator, or
- Drink water at every meal instead of soda.

In short, see the world from the perspective of the new person you're becoming and behave accordingly as often as possible.

4. Think of the reasons your beliefs are accurate

Another activity you can engage in on a regular basis is to list all the reasons your beliefs *are* accurate. For instance, if your new belief is "I can always become better", you can list the reasons that demonstrate this belief is true.

I can always become better because:

- I have access to tons of resources online and can learn from them,
- I can keep practicing and learning from feedback,
- I can find mentors or coaches who will help me improve,
- I can join mastermind groups with people who will inspire me,
- I've already improved in many ways and can repeat that process,
- I can work on my weaknesses, and so on.

47

As you repeatedly think of the reasons your beliefs are true, you'll begin to integrate them more deeply into your life.

5. Remind yourself of the reasons you want your beliefs to be true

Even if you don't really think your new belief is perfectly accurate, you can still find reasons to reinforce it to make it "truer". For instance, if you want to develop more determination, but don't believe you have any, think of past examples that demonstrate your determination and "grit".

I'm tenacious because:

- As a teenager, I worked odd jobs for months to save up for that one thing I really wanted,
- I failed that exam three times, but I kept taking it until I finally passed,
- I kept practicing the piano until I was able to play that difficult song, and so on.

The point is, you might not be convinced of your new belief yet, but there are most likely elements in your life that lead in that direction. Find them and list them all. As you do so, you'll realize that this belief is truer than you imagined, or it has the potential to become true over time.

By following the steps above, you'll begin to integrate your new beliefs and behave accordingly.

In the next section, we'll review the key beliefs you can adopt to leverage the power of belief and achieve almost anything you desire. You can use the above process to integrate them.

PART III

BUILDING FUNDAMENTAL BELIEFS

There is a difference between wishing for a thing and being ready to receive it. No one is ready for a thing, until he believes he can acquire it. The state of mind must be belief, not mere hope or wish.

— NAPOLEON HILL, AUTHOR.

Anything you accomplish in your life is largely determined by the beliefs you hold. When you rely on empowering beliefs that serve you well, you'll be well-positioned to design the life of your dreams. Conversely, if you hold onto limiting beliefs, you will struggle to truly express yourself and do all the things you ever dreamed of, as we saw in **PART II**. This is why adopting the right set of beliefs is essential.

In this section, we'll go over the fundamental beliefs that will enable you to navigate through the world with a high level of confidence. Once you internalize these beliefs, the way you think, feel and act will begin to change. You will build more confidence, develop more determination and open yourself up to a new world of possibilities.

Shall we start and make these new beliefs work for you?

7
___

THE NUMBER ONE META-BELIEF THAT RULES THEM ALL

 When you are able to control the movements of your attention in the subjective world, you can modify or alter your life as you please.

— NEVILLE GODDARD, AUTHOR OF, *THE POWER OF AWARENESS*.

Have you ever wondered whether we're living in an objective or a subjective world (i.e., a world that exists only because we perceive it)? The truth is, we can only ever perceive the world through our own eyes. Consequently, we can't say for sure the world would exist if *we* didn't exist.

Imagine if you chose to believe that the world is subjective and that you can use your thoughts to shape your reality. How would your outlook on life change as you began to see yourself as the ultimate creator of the world around you? Now, you might be a skeptic. You might think that it is nonsense, and it may very well be. However, the power of this meta-belief isn't in its accuracy; it's in the new way you begin to think, and the new actions you take as a result of making that belief part of your identity.

The moment you choose to believe you can change your reality by altering your thoughts is the moment you gain control over your life. This is when you start to shape your own destiny. You don't see yourself as a victim but as a victor. You stop feeling powerless and start feeling powerful instead.

To use the power of belief, you must recognize your ability to create a subjective world that will influence the objective world. Although this process will take time, as you gradually replace your current beliefs with more empowering ones, your confidence will grow. Equipped with new, powerful beliefs, you will spot new opportunities, meet different people, and come up with innovative ideas. And by doing so, you'll influence the world around you, creating a reality that is better aligned with your desires.

The bottom line is, you must believe that your thoughts will inevitably change your environment. This is how you will begin to utilize the power of belief.

1. Subjective reality leads to absolute responsibility

As you integrate the meta-belief that you largely become what you think about, you will feel compelled to take more responsibility for your actions. Understanding your thoughts will shape your reality. You will strive to cultivate better thoughts rather than continue blaming people or circumstances for your failures.

For instance:

- Instead of complaining about your job, you'll think of ways to improve your work situation. As you do so, things will start changing.
- Instead of hanging out with negative people, you'll think of the type of people you want to be around. As you keep doing so, you'll create opportunities to meet such people.
- Instead of reacting to your day, you'll become more proactive, which will enable you to feel more in control of your life.

A good analogy to illustrate the concept of subjective reality might be the movie "The Matrix". In this movie, when the hero, Neo, realizes the world he lives in isn't real, he suddenly unleashes his true power using his mind to transcend all artificial limitations. In one famous scene, we can even see him stop bullets. Of course, in the world we live in, the laws of physics make such deeds impossible. However, this movie is a great metaphor for the limitations we impose on ourselves, which have rendered us powerless. These limitations have made us settle for mediocrity instead of striving for and reaching our dreams.

Therefore, learn to use your subjective reality to create the objective reality you want to live in. Release your limitations. Remove all feelings of victimhood. Stop seeking commiseration. Then, implement the most empowering beliefs possible until they become unshakeable beliefs that drive every single one of your actions.

Remember, you can always adopt new beliefs and create thoughts that will lead you to behave differently. As the saying goes, doing the same things and expecting different results is a sign of insanity. Similarly, operating under the same old belief will bring about the same results over and over again. If you don't like the results you've obtained so far, change your beliefs.

Now that you've begun to understand the power of the meta-belief that rules them all (i.e., your thoughts shape your reality), let's introduce more fundamental beliefs you should adopt if you are to construct a powerful model of reality and navigate the world with greater confidence.

* * *

Action step

Imagine that your thoughts create your reality. If this is true, what new thoughts could you adopt to design a better reality?

Write down your answers in your action guide.

SEVEN CORE BELIEFS THAT WILL TRANSFORM YOUR LIFE

Belief #1—The universe is on your side

What's the point of trying if you believe everything is against you? If this is the way you think, you'll have a really difficult time attaining the long-term results you desire.

One of the foundational beliefs you must adopt to develop unshakeable confidence is the understanding that the universe is on your side. Things aren't happening *to* you, but *for* you.

Imagine if such a belief was at the core of everything you did. How would this improve the quality of your existence?

Anything you experience is what I call feedback from reality. Sometimes, this feedback is positive, and you obtain great results. But, more often than not, this feedback is negative, and your expectations are crushed.

For instance, when I started my personal development blog back in 2013, I naively thought my articles would go viral and thousands, if not millions, of people would read them. This is not what happened. Traffic remained extremely low and comments were non-existent. During the first few years, my expectations were crushed dozens of times. It wasn't a pleasant feeling. I could have seen it as a sign to give up. Instead, I viewed it as an invitation to humble myself, let go of expectations and realign with reality. I chose to keep working on my craft and pursued that path until I figured things out.

What about you? In what way(s) is the universe on your side? What is it trying to communicate to you? What lessons does it want you to learn before it lets you move forward?

When you believe the universe is conspiring to help you become happier and more successful, you will start seeing things differently. Every failure becomes a lesson to learn from, and every experience becomes an invitation to improve so that you can be a better version of yourself.

You can choose to believe the universe is on your side. This belief alone has the potential to transform your life.

* * *

Action step

Using your action guide, write down two or three challenges you're currently facing. Also, write down how you would perceive them differently if you believed the universe was on your side.

Belief #2—If others can, I can

Another foundational belief is, if other people can, you can too. We often believe others are better than us. We put successful people on a pedestal, while denying ourselves the possibility that we can achieve similar results. However, this is often not the case. We have our own strengths and weaknesses, but if others can do something, we can do it too. We are as capable as they are. Perhaps, we just failed to realize how hard they worked.

When I lived in Japan, people would often tell me I was smart just because I could speak Japanese well. If only they could be that smart, they would be fluent in English too (many Japanese study English).

But, is this statement true? Am I that smart? Sure, I do enjoy learning foreign languages and might be good at it. However, there is one tiny detail they failed to acknowledge—the insane number of hours I spent studying! Over the years, I must have studied Japanese for something like 20,000 hours. To put things in perspective, that's the equivalent of studying six hours every single day for almost ten years. Meanwhile, most Japanese people who study English only do so for a few hours a week at best. Then they wonder why they aren't fluent after a few months' worth of study.

The point is, if you put in the work, you can become good and often great at anything you desire. Remember, almost everything is a skill. You can become a competent writer, an effective speaker or an outstanding salesperson. You can learn how to create a business, market a product, coach people or manage a team. Or you can improve your cooking, driving or dancing skills. Pretty much anything others can do, you can too.

Remember, most people aren't nearly as smart as you think. They may have natural strengths or abilities you know nothing about—but so do you. I made one of my core beliefs that I'm as competent as anyone else, and it benefited me tremendously. Nowadays, I never miss an opportunity to remind myself that if others can, I can.

- If others can make money online, I can too.
- If others can become full-time writers I can too.
- If others can be confident, I can too.
- If others can deliver good speeches, I can too, and so on.

To sum things up, cultivate the habit of thinking that if someone else can, you can. Then, behave accordingly by taking the actions needed to improve your skills. You are only a few skills away from achieving your biggest goals. While you might not be as good as you want (yet), if you keep practicing, you eventually will be.

* * *

Action step

Using your action guide, write down three things other people are doing that you wish you could do too (for instance, speaking a foreign language, delivering speeches, playing an instrument well, et cetera). Now, realize that if others can, you can too.

Belief #3—You can always improve

Do you feel as though you aren't good enough? Do you doubt your ability to learn a new skill or gain the experience you need to make progress toward your goals?

We all fall prey to doubts. We all wonder whether we can complete a difficult project or achieve an ambitious goal. But our temporary self-doubts don't have to stop us from building confidence and achieving our biggest goals over time.

Another fundamental belief you must adopt is the belief you can improve. Your aptitudes are not limited or set in stone. Your potential isn't maxed out yet. You still have plenty of room to improve. Consequently, rather than feeling you're not good enough, understand that you're not good enough *yet*. The "yet" here is key. It changes your perspective. Instead of focusing on the "not good enough", you will focus on the "not yet" part. Instead of suffering from your current situation, you will become excited about what lies ahead of you. You will begin to enjoy the process of continuous improvement. You will think over the longer term and keep improving day after day. Yes, you're probably right: you're not good enough to achieve your biggest goals *yet*, but you eventually will be. This is inevitable.

Note that there are only two main things standing between you and your dreams:

1. Empowering beliefs you haven't yet fully integrated, and
2. A set of skills you haven't yet developed.

Now you can shrink and accept your current reality or expand and work on building your ideal future. I would recommend the latter.

And the only way to do this is by developing the skills, building the habits, cultivating the right mindset and taking the actions required to reach your destination.

Tom Bilyeu, founder of the popular podcast *Impact Theory*, invites us to develop an "anti-fragile" identity around learning. He argues that, instead of trying to avoid making mistakes, we should judge ourselves based on how much we're learning. When we do so, every setback we face makes us stronger. Obstacles become opportunities to grow. Failures become ways to remove our flaws. As we embrace the identity of a perpetual learner, we will inevitably move closer to our goals each day.

Therefore, see yourself as an unstoppable learner and take pride in each of your accomplishments. Build your identity around the concept of learning and self-improvement. Then, strive to learn more and learn faster. Ask better questions. React more constructively to feedback. Consume higher quality information. Surround yourself with smarter people. In short, do whatever it takes to learn as effectively and as quickly as possible.

Personally, I tell myself that I can learn anything I set my mind to, and I can do so faster than anybody else. Is this true? Probably not, but thinking this way motivates me to learn and acquire the skills I need to achieve my goals.

You can do the same. You can choose to see yourself as one of the fastest learners in the world. Once you do so, begin to evaluate yourself based on:

- How fast you can learn, and
- How willing you are to appear ignorant and face ridicule as you learn new skills.

When your identity becomes tied to your willingness to learn, you'll stop trying to look good, and you'll let go of your desire to appear smarter than you are. Instead, you'll humble yourself, knowing this is the best strategy to learn fast and achieve any goal you want.

The bottom line is, while you might not be good enough yet, this is only temporary. Perhaps, you had a slow start, but that's not the end of your story. *You are* an unstoppable learner. You will inevitably improve over time. Therefore, whatever you want to learn, do the work and never doubt your ability to learn the skills you need to travel from where you are to where you want to be.

* * *

Action step

Acknowledge that you can always improve. Then, in your action guide, write down all the reasons you can become better.

Belief #4—If you can do something once, you can repeat the process

What if you knew with absolute certainty that if you could do a task one time, you could replicate your success almost endlessly. How much would that boost your confidence?

Here is the truth: if you can do something one time, you can do it again.

All too often, we doubt our ability to perform the tasks we need to do the most. We wonder whether we can replicate past successes, and we forget how resourceful we truly are. While this is understandable, it is much more empowering to assume that if you can do something once you can do it over and over. This is how I think:

- If I can find one coaching client, then I can find ten, twenty, or fifty clients.
- If I can write one book, I can write one more, and one more.
- If I can make one dollar online, I can make one thousand dollars, ten thousands dollars or even a million dollars online.
- If I can make my first speech in public then I can make hundreds more.

Using the power of belief involves knowing deep down you can find the courage to do the things you dream of doing. No matter how hard something may be, you can always do it just one time. And once you've done it once you can repeat the process again and again until you achieve the results you desire.

Therefore, the only thing you need to do is to take that one action or accomplish that one task standing between you and your dreams —*just one time*. Then, assume you can do it again.

* * *

Action step

Complete the exercise below using your action guide:

- Think of one challenging thing you haven't been able to do (yet).
- Then realize you can do it just one time. Even if you can't do it right now, at least you can take one small step in that direction.
- Finally, understand that, if you can do that thing just once, you'll be able to do it again.

Belief #5—You can figure things out

Within yourself, you have the ability to figure things out. This ability to find solutions to your problems is inherent to being human and can never be taken away from you. If you currently feel powerless, it may be that you haven't learned to trust yourself enough to believe you can solve your problems.

The point is, humans are natural problem solvers. We are designed to find innovative ways to solve challenges. Therefore, one of the most empowering beliefs we can adopt is the belief we can figure things out. Whatever challenges we may be facing, know that we're resourceful enough to find a solution. And if we can't find a solution, it's not a problem, but something we must accept and live with.

Now, having the ability to figure things out doesn't mean you must solve your problems all by yourself. In fact, in many cases, the solution lies in asking people for help or copying what someone else did before you.

Also, note that many of your problems can be solved through action. Therefore, when you notice yourself ruminating instead of taking concrete action to solve your problems, remember that thinking alone is rarely enough to solve your challenges. Thought must be followed by action.

You can figure things out. This fundamental belief will enable you to solve your problems and achieve your future goals. Remember, if others can, you can too. If they can figure things out, so can you.

* * *

Action steps

Using your action guide, complete the following exercise:

- Write down one major problem you're currently facing.
- Then, write down everything you could do to solve it.

Belief #6—Failure is inevitable

No successful human being was ever able to accomplish anything significant without facing repeated failures. Consequently, failure isn't something to dread or to avoid at all cost, but something to learn from. The difference between successful people and unsuccessful ones is often determined by the meaning they give to "failure". Successful people embrace failure and perceive every setback as a learning opportunity. They use failures as feedback to improve their knowledge and move closer to their goals. Conversely, other people tend to be afraid of failure and do whatever they can to avoid it.

This is not surprising since we've all been taught to dread failures. The school system didn't reward us for trying, but for giving the correct answers. However, in many situations, there is no such thing as a "correct" answer. Life isn't a test with multiple answers to choose from, it is much more complicated than that. For instance, when pursuing a goal, many parameters must be taken into consideration, parameters such as timing, experience, personality traits, economic situation, luck, location and current skill levels.

To use the power of belief effectively, you must understand the concept that short-term failures are not only inevitable but also necessary. Then, you must change your belief around failure.

Most people take failures personally. They perceive them as proof of their inadequacy. But this is an inaccurate perception of reality. There isn't failure on one side and success on the other. Both belong to the same process. Failure is merely reality telling you to adjust your trajectory so that you can achieve success (i.e., any goal you may have). It might encompass improving your skills, refining your approach, fine-tuning your strategy, asking for help or trying one more time.

In truth, reality doesn't care how often you "fail". It won't stop you nor punish you if you encounter too many setbacks. If anything, it will help you succeed by giving you additional feedback which you can use to adjust your trajectory. For instance, entrepreneurs who failed at multiple ventures are more likely to succeed next time around (provided they learn from their mistakes, of course).

People who achieve higher levels of success have failed far more often than the average person ever will. This is how they became successful. If you want to achieve major goals, you must adopt the core belief that failure is inevitable. Don't fail for the sake of it though. Fail in a way that allows you to receive invaluable feedback. Then, use this feedback to adjust your trajectory until you finally hit your target.

When I look back at my writing career, it felt as though I failed at most of the things I tried. I spent countless hours writing articles few people read. I wrote books that didn't make any money and it took me two to three years before I could earn a decent living. I kept failing until one day I woke up realizing I had actually become fairly successful.

The bottom line is, failure is a natural part of the success process. You're never really failing; you're actually running experiments to gather valuable feedback. Therefore, the key is not to avoid failure, but to make sure that the experiments you run are sound and move you closer to your goals.

* * *

Action step

Using your action guide, complete the exercise below:

- Write down one big "failure" in your life.

Then, answer the following questions:

- What did I learn from it?
- What's good about it?
- What positive things did it lead to (mindset change, new opportunities, invaluable lessons learned, et cetera)?

Belief #7—Your success is inevitable

Failure is inevitable, but so is success. The more you fail, the more likely you are to succeed. Armed with the fundamental beliefs mentioned previously, you now understand why success might be inevitable for you. As a reminder, these core beliefs are:

- You can use your thoughts to shape your reality,
- If others can, you can,
- You can always improve,
- If you can do something once, you can do it again,
- You can figure things out, and
- Failure is inevitable (and leads to long-term success).

Once you truly believe success is inevitable, you'll begin to think, feel and act differently. You'll be much more determined and much more committed to achieving the goals you're pursuing. That's the power of this belief.

Now, I'm not saying it will be easy. In fact, to reach extraordinary goals, you must develop an extraordinary mindset. But as you learn to use the power of belief more effectively, over time, you'll find yourself obtaining impressive results. So, start believing success is inevitable. Live in that "truth" every day and see how things change for you.

* * *

Action step

Adopt the belief that success is inevitable by reminding yourself of the following:

- You can use your thoughts to shape your reality,
- If others can, you can too,
- You can always improve,
- If you can do something once, you can do it again,
- You can figure things out, and
- Short-term failure is inevitable and leads to long-term success.

PART IV

THE BELIEF FORMULA

I believe we create our own lives. And we create it by our thinking, feeling patterns in our belief system. I think we're all born with this huge canvas in front of us and the paintbrushes and the paint, and we choose what to put on this canvas.

— LOUISE L. HAY, AUTHOR.

Instead of doubting yourself, what if you had a specific formula you could use to develop unshakeable confidence? How would that make you feel? How would it change your life for the better?

In this section, we'll cover The Belief Formula which you can apply to build greater and more powerful self-confidence. We'll see:

- How you can design an empowering environment that will boost your self-confidence,
- How you can take repeated action to transform your reality,
- Why having an intense desire is essential, and
- Why being willing to face discomfort is key.

The Belief Formula is as follows:

Empowering environment + repeating action + intense desire + willingness to face discomfort = unshakeable belief.

Let's explain briefly each component of this formula:

Empowering environment. This is putting yourself in a favorable environment that enables you to perform at your best. It entails:

- Creating a positive mental environment through effective conditioning (affirmations, visualization, self-talk),
- Surrounding yourself with a supportive peer group (positive friends, mentors, coaches), and
- Building a physical environment that facilitates positive actions while making undesirable behaviors harder to engage in (i.e., removing junk food from your house, putting your goals on your desk, et cetera).

Repeated action. Taking action can solve a lot of problems including a lack of self-confidence. It is what allows you to reinforce your core beliefs so you can cultivate greater confidence over time. Among other things, taking repeated actions means:

- Choosing to think better thoughts *every day* until you see manifestations of these thoughts in the real world (see also *The Meta-belief that rules them all*),
- Continuously acting in accordance with the idea that the universe is on your side and gathering evidence that supports that belief (see also *Belief #1—The Universe is on your side*),
- Pursuing your goals *relentlessly*, knowing that if others can you can, and, by doing so, obtain results that reinforce that belief (see also *Belief #2—If others can, so can you*),
- Working on your craft *tirelessly*, knowing that you can always get better and, as you do so, experience that truth first-hand (see also *Belief #3—You can always become better*), and
- Trying *as many times as needed* until you achieve one key task such as landing your first client, delivering your first speech or making your first sale. Then, taking more actions once

you realize you can replicate your early results (See also *Belief #4—If you can do something once, you can do it over and over again*).

Intense desire. Desire is key to any achievement. You must understand why believing in yourself and in your vision is so important, so that you can strengthen your conviction and boost your confidence over time. Without desire, you won't feel compelled to take consistent action and, as a result, you won't achieve any significant results.

Willingness to face discomfort. Fear and discomfort are mostly illusions created by your mind. The repeated exposure to fear through concrete action enables you to get a glimpse of your true nature (i.e., the confident and capable person you inherently are as a human being). As you begin to face your fears, you will access a new world of opportunity, realizing that what you thought impossible might not be.

These four factors (empowering environment, repeated action, intense desire, and willingness to face discomfort) cannot fail to skyrocket your confidence. And they are all within your control. This is why belief is an inner game. It's a game played between you and you. Nothing else stands in your way. Apply these four factors diligently and your confidence will inevitably grow.

Now, does that mean it will be easy? Of course not. But you can do it because, like any other human being, you possess the power of belief. And, like anyone else, you can activate this power using *The Belief Formula*.

Let's go over each of these components in greater depth to see how you can start putting them into practice.

9

EMPOWERING ENVIRONMENT

For most of us, believing in ourselves isn't something that happens naturally. Our level of self-belief is largely determined by the environment we put ourselves into. This environment can work for or against us. It can inspire us and help us stay confident, or it can demotivate us and make us feel powerless.

What about you? What does your current environment look like? Is it working for you or against you?

To develop unshakeable belief, you must become more conscious of your environment and take the necessary steps to design an empowering environment that enables you to perform at your best. Your environment is critical because it becomes the source of the information that penetrates your mind (often without your consent). Roughly speaking, we can identify three types of environment:

1. Your mental environment,
2. Your social environment, and
3. Your physical environment.

Let's look at each of these individually, shall we?

1. Your mental environment

Your mental environment consists of your thought process and the emotions you experience as a result of it.

When you entertain good thoughts, you'll feel good and will be better equipped to achieve your goals. Conversely, when you fall prey to too many negative thoughts, you'll experience negative feelings such as shame, guilt, anger or fear. These negative emotions will prevent you from taking the actions necessary to reach your goals and design the life you want.

This is why you must train your mind to experience more positive emotions. Remember, the power of belief is accessible *at all times*, but to bring that power into existence you must choose to condition your mind accordingly.

In this regard, we can compare our mind to a programmable computer. Unfortunately, rather than programming our mind proactively, most of us have been programmed by our experiences and by others. We let other people and life circumstances dictate how we should think, feel and behave. We allow our past to determine our self-image. Of course, this happens largely unconsciously, starting during our childhood.

a. Reprogramming your mind

To reprogram your mind, you must replace disempowering thoughts with empowering ones. By consciously choosing new thoughts, you can begin to implement new thinking patterns and rewire your brain.

To do so, you must use the power of repetition and expose yourself to the same empowering beliefs over and over again. You've let false beliefs penetrate your mind without your consent, and you must now recondition your mind to work *for* you, rather than *against* you.

A simple yet effective way to reprogram your mind is to expose yourself to positive content every day. For instance, when he was a university student, the personal development blogger, Steve Pavlina, decided to graduate in three semesters instead of the usual four years. To help him achieve this goal, he chose to listen to educational audiobooks for at least two hours a day. Doing so allowed him to program his mind to perform at his best while remaining optimistic and enabled him to achieve his goal.

Similarly, during the years I tried to make it as a blogger and writer, I kept filling my mind with positivity every day. This enabled me to maintain a positive attitude and keep persevering. Today, I still feed my mind with positivity on a consistent basis.

Being exposed to inspirational or educational content over and over will inevitably begin to affect your thought process. You can think of it as positive "brainwashing". Many malevolent religious gurus use repetition to manipulate their members. Some parents use brainwashing to turn their children against their spouse after a nasty divorce. Both of these are examples of conditioning and show how effective it can be (for better or for worse).

* * *

Action step

In your action guide, write down what you could do every day to maintain a positive emotional state.

b. Repeating powerful affirmations

An effective way to rewire your brain is by repeating positive affirmations. Affirmations are phrases you say to yourself to orient your thinking and internalize the specific beliefs to help you create your ideal future. You can use affirmations to reprogram your mind, to boost your emotional state, and to develop greater confidence.

Most successful and happy people understand the power of words and use them to their advantage. They're careful with their words and avoid affirming to themselves anything they don't want to become true. For instance:

- They don't tell themselves they are stupid. Instead, they say to themselves they're smart enough to figure things out.
- They don't tell themselves they aren't capable of doing something. Instead, they repeat to themselves they're resourceful enough to find a solution.
- They don't tell themselves they are busy. Instead, they remind themselves they have enough time to do the things that truly matter.

So, beware of your own conditioning. If your programming tells you that you don't deserve to be happy, then you'll act accordingly and will struggle to find happiness. If your programming tells you that you can't grow past your current abilities, then you won't make any effort to develop new skills.

The same way you upgrade your phone to get new features, you must upgrade your mind proactively, by implementing the beliefs you need to build your ideal life.

- Do you tend to give up too quickly? Upgrade your mind and create the new identity of someone who perseveres no matter what.
- Do you feel as though you're not good enough? Keep telling yourself you can become better at whatever you desire, while acknowledging all the things you're doing well.
- Do you feel powerless? Program your mind by reminding yourself that the universe is on your side and that you can use your thoughts to change your reality.

Bear in mind that if you don't affirm to yourself who you are or want to be, then you'll let your unconscious habits or external circumstances decide it for you. Consequently, start affirming who you want to be and reprogram your mind to perform at your best. Because if you don't, nobody else can or will ever do it for you.

* * *

Action step

Using your action guide, come up with a couple of affirmations you could repeat every day to develop a stronger mindset.

To learn how to create affirmations, revisit *Part II. Identifying your limiting beliefs, section C. Integrating your new beliefs - I. Writing down your empowering beliefs.*

c. Using the power of visualization

When you visualize, you momentarily escape the present to live in the ideal future you want to create. Rather than being a victim of your present thoughts and feelings, choose to think better thoughts and create better feelings. By doing this, you begin to create the necessary conditions to manifest a new reality that matches the person you aspire to become.

In other words, visualization is a way to tell the world that you do not accept your present reality anymore and that you are ready to use the power of belief to change it. When backed up with intense desire and strong conviction, this becomes one of the most powerful forces for change.

What about you? Are you making the most of your imagination? Are you using the power of belief to shape your future?

How to visualize

You might see visualization as something foreign or even mystical. You might be thinking, "But I don't know how to visualize". In truth, however, you're using visualization every day. Visualizing is simply the act of putting your attention toward something that doesn't exist in the present. In fact, this is what we spend most of our time doing. We worry about a future that hasn't happened yet (and often never will), and we dwell on a past that is long gone. The difference is that, in these particular cases, we're engaging in negative visualization—a type of visualization that is not structured nor performed with a clear intention.

Here are a few simple steps to help you get started with visualization:

1) Relax

The more relaxed you are, the more effective visualization will be. As you put yourself in a deep state of relaxation, you will gain better access to your subconscious. As a result, your subconscious will accept what you visualize more readily and without the mental noise and objections you often receive from your conscious mind. Also, remember that your mind is at its most receptive first thing in the morning and last thing at night. These are great times to practice visualization.

2) Visualize what you want

Your imagination is limitless. Therefore, there is no situation you cannot create in your mind. Whatever you decide to visualize, try to make it as specific and clear as possible. An effective way to do this is by creating a mental movie. Put yourself inside the movie and make it appear as though it's happening right here, right now.

Consider it this way: when you think of past events, do you remember specific memories or just fixed images? You need to create mental movies similar to the memories you would have if what you desire had already happened or was actually happening. For example, if you want to travel the world, don't just list the name of the countries you want to visit, actually see yourself walking the streets, visiting famous monuments and eating in local restaurants. Be specific. Where are you staying? What are you eating? Who are you with?

Visualizing is not merely daydreaming. The "One day I will" type of thinking seldom, if ever, materializes. Daydreaming is nothing more than wishful thinking. Conversely, with visualization, there is desire and commitment. It doesn't mean you need to be tense or stressed about it, though. Just relax and trust that your desire and commitment will help you reach your goals.

3) Feel as though you're already there

Emotions drive actions. When you feel good, you're more creative, more resourceful and more productive. When you're in a positive frame of mind, you readily take the actions you need to achieve your goals. Therefore, whenever you visualize, engage as many of your emotions as possible. Feel excited about your vision. More specifically, feel as though you are already the person you want to be, and you already have the things you want. For instance, if you want to be confident, see yourself being confident in a variety of situations. Create a mental movie and revisit it over and over again. Feel confident while you make a presentation at work. See yourself relaxed as you attend a social event. Imagine people around you being friendly and receptive.

Feelings are important because they allow you to shift your beliefs quickly and profoundly. As your beliefs change, your subconscious will try to align the reality around you with your new reality. As a result, you'll find yourself taking more action to close the gap between where you are and where you believe you must be.

If you feel any resistance when you visualize, acknowledge it, let it go and refocus on the object of your visualization.

4) Focus on what you want as often as possible

Here again, repetition is key. Spend time every day visualizing the person you want to become. Step into your vision first thing in the morning and see yourself as the person you want to be. Keep visualizing this same thing throughout the day. Then, do the same at night before going to bed. Keep feeling as though you're already that person. Assume that the qualities you are trying to develop are already inside you, waiting to be uncovered.

The repetition of an emotionalized vision will lead you to take different actions. Over time, these new actions will move you closer to the person you want to become.

These are the four simple steps to effective visualization.

The bottom line is this: you can tap into your imagination 24/7. Therefore, make sure you use it to create your ideal life, not to revisit unhappy memories or worry about your future. What you think about often enough and for long enough will tend to become your reality—but only if you take action, of course. Thus, keep visualizing your ideal life and act every day so as to move closer to it.

* * *

Action step

Practice visualization every day when you wake and/or when you go to bed. Using the steps described above.

2. Social environment

Many of our beliefs are created through our interactions with other people. During these interactions, others influence us, passing onto us some of their beliefs. It's no surprise that the people we spend time with significantly impact the way we see ourselves and the world.

Weak-minded people are easily influenced. They may change their beliefs or adjust their behaviors just to win people's approval. For example, they may let one negative comment stop them from doing something they really want to do. Such behavior results from their ignorance of the power of belief and how they could use it to improve their life.

On the other hand, strong-minded people make their environment work for them. They understand the need to use it to strengthen their self-belief. As a result, they choose to surround themselves with positive people who will strengthen their power of belief rather than negative people who will take it from them.

Remember that while the power of belief is always within you, you must still strive to create an empowering environment that will support your goals and boost your confidence. This entails surrounding yourself with positive people. The better your "social environment" is, the easier it will be to activate the power of belief and maintain unshakeable belief long term.

For instance, you are more likely to succeed as an entrepreneur if you spend time with successful entrepreneurs. You'll be able to encourage each other and persevere during tough times. Alternatively, if you surround yourself with people who don't have an entrepreneurial mindset, you might struggle to obtain similar results. Your friends may tell you that you're not going to make it. They may ask you why your progress is so slow, or they may offer advice to you on subjects they know nothing about.

The point is, your environment can make you or break you. To get the most out of life, you must move from a disempowering environment to an empowering one. Being around negative people is like driving a car with the brakes on. It will limit your potential and prevent you from reaching your biggest goals.

It is often said, we are the average of the five people we spend the most time with. Would you rather be around pessimistic people who've given up on their dreams and would like you to do the same with yours, or be around growth-oriented people who move toward their dreams with unstoppable optimism while supporting yours?

How to meet the right people

Now let's look at a few things you can do to surround yourself with the right people.

1. **Identify the type of people you want to be around.** The more specific you are the better. What are these people doing? How do they behave? How are they thinking? Where are they likely to hang out?
2. **Identify the acquaintance(s) you'd like to spend more time with.** Think of the network of people you know. Is there someone you'd like to spend more time with, or do you know someone who knows that type of person?
3. **See yourself as bigger than your current environment.** Start seeing yourself as the person you want to be. Imagine yourself being in the ideal environment. Start acting like the people you'd love to be around. If they're disciplined, build more discipline. If they read books, read more books. If they challenge themselves to grow and become better, do the same thing. As you keep thinking and acting like the person

you want to be, over the long term, you'll be naturally presented with opportunities to meet like-minded people. Remember, as you change your thought process and take new actions, your environment will begin to change. It may be a gradual process that unfolds almost seamlessly, or it may be a sudden change resulting from drastic decisions you made (cutting off negative people, changing neighborhood, joining new groups, et cetera), but it is inevitable.

4. **Go to places where you're the most likely to find people you want to meet.** If you want to meet online entrepreneurs, attend an event for entrepreneurs or visit a city or neighborhood where thousands of them live. In today's hyper-connected world, you have no excuse not to meet the people you want to talk to.

5. **Join relevant groups and forums online.** If you can't meet people in real life, meet them online. For instance, I'm a member of groups for writers on Facebook. I find it to be beneficial and inspiring.

6. **Read books written by the people you'd like to meet or be like.** If you can't meet the people you want to meet (yet), read their books. It will help you change your mindset, making it more likely that you will meet these types of people in the future.

7. **Build your own tribe.** Finally, to attract the people you want to be around, you can also create a group. For instance, a couple of years ago, I contacted two writers who were on the same path as me and invited them to a mastermind group. What about you? What type of people would help you develop the right mindset and build the confidence needed to achieve your goals? And what group could you create to attract them?

To sum up, you must do whatever it takes to surround yourself with people who will bring the best out in you. Fortunately, doing so is within your power. As you change the way you think and clarify what you want, over time, your environment will change, and you will begin to attract the right people. Note that sometimes you might need to make drastic decisions such as moving to a different neighborhood or spending money to attend events where you'll be able to meet the right people.

Never forget that you can always change your "social environment". The best way to do this might be by focusing on your own personal growth until you become too "big" for your current environment. So, work on yourself until you outgrow your current environment.

* * *

Action step

Answer the following question using your action guide:

- What type of people do you want to be around?
- Is there a friend/acquaintance you'd like to spend more time with?
- Where are you the most likely to meet people you want to be around?
- Which relevant groups or forums could you join online?
- Which book(s) written by people you'd like to be could you read?
- Could you create your own tribe?

3. Physical environment

Changing your physical environment isn't just about being around the right people or feeding your mind with positivity. It's also about optimizing your environment to encourage desired behaviors and discourage unwanted ones. By making it easier to take the actions required to achieve the desired results, you'll be able to generate momentum and boost your confidence.

For instance:

- By removing junk food from your house, you'll encourage the desired behavior "I want to eat more healthily", while

discouraging unwanted behaviors, such as eating potato chips or drinking soda.
- By writing down your goals and displaying them prominently, you'll make it easier to refer to them daily and avoid becoming distracted by non-essential goals.
- By keeping your phone out of your bedroom, you reduce the potential to look at it first thing in the morning.
- By preparing your running gear the night before, you'll make it easier to exercise every morning.

Remember, our mind is always looking for the path of least resistance. It is lazy by nature and likes to maintain the status quo. To give you an example, when I write a book, I sometimes put the internet modem in a storage room. Now, while it would only take a few minutes to reclaim it, I don't. It just requires too much effort. Instead, I'd rather write (even though the process of writing requires probably far more mental energy). This is how lazy the mind can be. So why not use this characteristic to your advantage?

In short, by optimizing your environment to facilitate the desired behavior, you increase the chances you'll act the way you want to. Over time, just a couple of new behaviors applied consistently can have a major impact on your results and can significantly boost your self-confidence.

What about you? What specific things could you do to improve your physical environment?

* * *

Action step

Using your action guide, write down the specific things you could do to optimize your physical environment.

10

REPEATED ACTIONS

Action and confidence work hand in hand and are critical ingredients to success in any area of life. The more action you take toward your goals, the more self-belief you will cultivate, and the more self-belief you cultivate, the easier you'll find it to take action. Since you can always decide to take action, you can always strengthen your self-belief.

Lack of self-belief usually results from lack of self-trust (i.e., not seeing yourself as capable of doing what needs to be done). Therefore, an effective way to develop self-belief is to set and achieve small goals consistently. As you do so, your confidence will grow, and you'll find yourself able to complete bigger and more complex tasks.

Therefore, learn to trust yourself. See goals as promises you make to yourself. Rather than breaking these promises over and over as most people do, wherever possible, honor them every single time. In short, whenever you promise yourself to do something, do it. This is one of the most effective ways to build self-confidence.

1. The power of habits

Repeated actions also include habits. What you do every day creates small wins, boosts your confidence and, in the end, creates the necessary conditions for the achievement of major goals. By repeatedly thinking, feeling and acting a certain way, you develop great confidence or, conversely, undermine it. It all depends on what you think, feel and do.

Now, let's see how you can create rock-solid habits you can stick to over the long term.

a. How to create rock-solid habits

Adopting rock-solid habits is a great way to condition your mind to maintain a positive attitude, even during challenging times. Remember, your ability to maintain a positive emotional state will enable you to keep taking action repeatedly for months until you turn your thoughts into reality in the real world.

In this section, we'll see how you can implement powerful daily habits to boost your motivation and help you maintain a positive mindset. Few people truly realize that almost everything in life can be developed through repetition. Habits aren't just limited to meditating, exercising, or setting goals; they are much more than that. You can implement simple habits that, over the long term, will allow you to learn almost anything, such as:

- Boosting your creativity,
- Becoming decisive,
- Being more present,
- Building confidence,
- Developing charisma,
- Feeling more grateful,
- Thinking more critically, and so on.

For instance, you can enhance your creativity by coming up with ten new ideas every day on how to make money, increase your productivity, or serve your clients better. Alternatively, to boost your ability to be grateful, you can focus on the thing you're thankful for every morning.

Let me introduce seven habits that, I believe, are some of the most powerful ones you can adopt. Consider experimenting with at least a few of them.

Note that these habits will all help you take control of your emotional state. Why does this matter? Because your ability to condition your mind and manage your emotional state better is key to changing anything in your life. The better you feel, the more creative, resilient and productive you will become. As you feel better, you'll have more fuel in your emotional tank to move beyond your comfort zone and make positive changes in your life. If you've ever tried to make difficult changes when you were tired or depressed, you know how hard this can be.

Below are the seven habits I recommend you experiment with:

Habit #1—Set daily goals

Setting goals every day will dramatically boost your productivity. A simple way to set goals is to take a pen and a sheet of paper and make a list of three to five tasks you want to accomplish during the upcoming day. Once you've done this, prioritize your tasks by numbering them in order of importance. Begin by working on your first task and make sure to complete it before moving on to the next one. Then, repeat the process. If you can do this daily, you'll get a lot done.

Habit #2—Read your goals every day/week

You can easily forget about your goals when things are busy. Reading them daily is a great way to rectify this situation. In addition, make sure you take a moment to visualize your goals and to remind yourself how achieving them would make you feel.

Checking your goals every day will help you think long term and stay focused on what truly matters. In **PART V.** *Sustaining belief long-term,* we'll discuss in greater depth what you can do to become a long-term thinker and maintain your confidence over time.

Habit #3—Meditation

Meditation provides many benefits. For instance, meditating can help:

- Reduce worries,
- Lessen loneliness and depression,
- Increase focus,
- Enhance self-esteem,
- Improve the immune system, and
- Boost memory.

You can begin by spending just a few minutes a day. There are many ways to meditate, but it can be as simple as closing your eyes and focusing on your breathing. There are also several good books for beginners to help you get started.

Habit #4—Practice gratitude

Forgetting to express gratitude is a major cause of unhappiness. We tend to take everything for granted, failing to appreciate the little things in life (or even the big ones).

Every day during my morning ritual, I ask myself what I'm grateful for. I then spend a few minutes thinking about everything that crosses my mind, or I read through my gratitude journal, which consists of positive reviews I received for my books and compliments of all kinds.

Habit #5—Consume inspirational books and videos

Feeding your mind with inspirational material on a daily basis will help you stay motivated for the long haul. If you can't find the time to read, consider listening to audiobooks during your daily commute.

Habit #6—Self-reflection

Self-reflection is one of the best ways to supercharge your growth. Why not take a few minutes every evening to reflect upon your day?

Consider asking yourself the following questions:

- What did I do well today?
- What could I have done better?
- What can I learn from today?
- What will I do differently in the future?

Habit #7—Exercise daily

You already know you should exercise each day, but are you doing it? You don't need to buy fancy gym equipment or even buy a gym membership. Simple activities like walking or running can be enough, as is recommended in the following article on Harvard Medical School's website:

"As a rough guide, the current American Heart Association/American College of Sports Medicine standards call for able-bodied adults to do moderate-intensity exercise (such as brisk walking), for at least thirty minutes on five days each week or intense aerobic exercise (such as running), for at least twenty minutes three days each week."

The article further states:

"In a report that included findings from multiple well-done studies, researchers found that walking reduced the risk of cardiovascular events by 31% and cut the risk of dying by 32%. These benefits were equally robust in men and women. Protection was evident even at distances of just 5½ miles per week and at a pace as casual as about 2 miles per hour."

So, even if you hate physical activity, why not go for a walk every day? You can even use that time to feed your mind with educational and/or inspirational material by listening to audiobooks.

If you were to stick to one new habit every day, which one would make the biggest difference in your life over the long term?

b. How to implement habits that stick

Now, let's see briefly how to implement habits you can stick to over the long term.

1) Define your habits clearly

Define the new habits you want to implement with as much clarity as

85

possible. Make sure they are measurable (i.e., make sure you know whether you have performed them or not). For instance, they could include a specific number of repetitions (doing ten push-ups), or a duration (meditating for five minutes).

2) Start small

A good question to ask yourself is, "Am I confident I can stick to this habit every day even when I'm tired or when I don't feel like doing it?" The idea is to make your habit small enough to avoid self-sabotage, while staying consistent over the long term. For instance, you could decide to meditate for a couple of minutes or to go for a five-minute run.

3) Set triggers

It's easy to skip habits. To avoid doing so, make sure you have a clear trigger for your habits. A good example of a trigger is "waking up". For instance, you may decide to meditate as soon as you wake. Another example could be, "going to work". You may choose to visualize your ideal future as soon as you leave your house on your daily commute.

When setting triggers, the key is to make sure they are reliable. They should be something you do every day such as taking a shower, waking, eating breakfast or leaving home. You want them to act as anchors. If your triggers are inconsistent, you are more likely to forget about your daily habits.

So, what specific triggers will you use for your small habits?

4) Stack your habits

Another powerful method is to stack, or group, your habits together, which will prevent you from skipping them. For instance, you could implement a morning routine. I love morning routines which, I believe, are some of the most powerful activities you can do to improve your life. Imagine if you could stack the most powerful habits together and do all of them first thing in the morning? How would this change your life over time?

To give you an example, while writing this book, my morning ritual included:

- Getting out of bed immediately and smiling,
- Meditating for twenty minutes,
- Drinking two glasses of water,
- Stretching,
- Practicing gratitude,
- Setting goals for the day, and
- Writing for at least forty-five minutes.

Now it's your turn. How could you stack your habits together?

5) Undertake a 30-Day Challenge

30-Day Challenges can be incredibly powerful. This is because they encourage you to stay consistent and help you build momentum. Look at the habits you stacked together previously. Make them part of your morning ritual and commit to performing this ritual for at least the next thirty days. Then, see how it impacts your life.

Implementing daily habits will ensure that you make progress towards your goals every day, while conditioning your mind to stay in a positive state of mind day after day.

* * *

Action step

In your action guide, write down three (small) habits you want to implement. Then, stack them together and perform them each day for at least the next thirty days.

c. How to take greater action

With the democratization of the internet, we now have access to an enormous amount of information. There is one major issue though —most of us never put what we learn into action.

True confidence doesn't come from merely absorbing information, whether through reading books, watching YouTube videos, or taking online courses. These are just the tools we can use to accelerate our progress in the real world.

For instance, you won't become an exceptional public speaker just by reading books or watching videos on public speaking. It might help, but above anything else, you must practice speaking in public. Nor will you learn how to drive by reading books on how to drive. The same also applies for less tangible things such philosophy, economy, sociology, and other intellectual disciplines. To learn them effectively, you must generate output whether by taking notes, making presentations, or teaching someone else about a new concept you just learned.

In short, you must gain experience through actual practice. Obvious, right? Yet, that's not what most people do. They ponder, talk about what they plan to do or daydream about the future—but they fail to act.

The first step to becoming more action-oriented is to be honest with yourself and to separate true action from feel-good activities. True actions move you closer to your goal, give you experience and build your inner confidence. Feel-good activities give the illusion of progress, and are pleasant, but they don't help you achieve your goals or develop confidence.

True actions are often challenging or even scary. Examples of true actions include:

- Calling a prospect,
- Writing a book,
- Creating a product,
- Practicing a speech, or
- Playing a musical instrument.

Examples of feel-good activities are:

- Reading a book (if done passively),
- Watching a video (if done passively),

- Redesigning your website logo for the tenth time, or
- Holding meetings (when unnecessary).

The more action-oriented you become and the more often you complete the things that need to be completed, the more confidence you'll build and the bigger goals you'll be able to achieve over time.

Once you have identified your feel-good activities, the second step is to commit to taking more real actions while reducing those that only feel good. Confident people make things happen. Rather than making excuses or wasting time on trivial activities, they do the hard work. By spending their time and effort on high-impact tasks, they accomplish more while building greater confidence in the process.

Also, confident people handpick the information they consume. When they read a book or take a course, it is with the intention of applying it right away. This approach safeguards them from falling for "analysis paralysis"—a phenomenon that can occur when we don't do anything with the information we gather. Analysis paralysis often leads people to feel overwhelmed. It creates a gap between theoretical knowledge and actual experience. In other words, people accumulate "knowledge" but fail to gain first-hand experience. By not taking enough action, they don't get enough feedback from reality. As a result, they feel stuck, unable to identify:

- What works from what doesn't,
- What they should do more of and what they should do less of, or
- The skills they need to develop.

This is why taking action is critical. It allows you to discover what works and what doesn't. It develops skills thought habituation, and it creates a trail you can follow. If you lack confidence or feel stuck, it's probably because you're not taking enough action.

Many people reading self-help books like this one are information addicts. Believing they need more information, they keep reading and reading, hoping they'll find the magic pill that will accelerate their success. There is one problem though—this magic pill doesn't exist. While there are many things people can do to achieve results faster, in the end they still need to take concrete action. There is no way around this fact.

Alternatively, some people use "learning" as an excuse to procrastinate without feeling guilty about it. They pat themselves on the back for taking action (i.e., learning), but are they really taking action?

I used to be an information addict. However, a few years ago, I realized all the books I had read hadn't helped drive the changes I wanted in my life. I might have read hundreds of books and acquired a great deal of "knowledge" but what did I use it for? Some of my friends, who probably never read a self-help book, seem happier and/or more successful than I was. Something needed to change.

So, I became obsessed with taking action. I wanted to share what I learned. I wanted to improve my life and be in a position to help others. Even though I didn't feel ready, I started writing articles and later on, books. I set small goals and achieved them. I began to consume less information and produce more content. I talked less and did more. This shift in mindset has allowed me to write over twenty books in the past five years. But, more importantly, it built my confidence and made me feel as though I was doing what I was supposed to do.

Perhaps you can relate to my story? If so, practice reducing the amount of information you consume (books, videos, online courses, seminars, et cetera). It might even be a good idea to go on an information diet and focus only on taking action in the coming two to four weeks. To do so, stop buying books and stop watching videos. Instead, focus on your most important project. Then take action, and only read books or attend courses when absolutely necessary.

The more action you take, the more progress you'll make, and the more confidence you will develop over time.

The point is, you can turn yourself into an action taker. You can increase your speed of implementation and generate better results faster. As you do so, you'll begin to develop unshakeable self-confidence and belief. You'll find yourself breaking through your mental barriers and achieving bigger and bigger goals.

Remember, confidence is a skill and, when you do the right things, developing more of it is inevitable. One of these things is "simply" to take more action.

* * *

Action step

Complete the exercise below using the action guide:

- Select one major goal you're currently working on.
- Make a list of the actions you're taking to reach it (use the table to separate true actions from feel-good activities).
- Practice taking more effective actions (a good idea is to incorporate them into your morning ritual whenever possible).

11

INTENSE DESIRE

66 The desire which realizes itself is always a desire upon which attention is exclusively concentrated, for an idea is endowed with power only in proportion to the degree of attention fixed on it.

— NEVILLE GODDARD, AUTHOR, *THE POWER OF
AWARENESS*.

Everything starts with desire. You act because you desire something, whether it is better health, more fulfilling relationships, financial abundance or a deeper sense of contribution to your community. Desire allows you to activate the power of belief. When you desire something strongly enough, you are compelled to develop the confidence required to obtain that thing. You now have a big enough reason why you must cultivate self-belief.

For instance, if you truly want to become an engineer, you'll begin to act in a way that will lead you to achieve that goal. You'll study hard, find mentors, buy books, or attend courses or work with private teachers. In short, you'll take massive and intensive action to move closer to your goals.

Conversely, if you have only a mild interest in something, you won't feel compelled to act, and even if you do, your level of action will likely be insufficient to generate decent results. This is what happens to many people. Not having a strong enough desire, they're unwilling to invest the time and energy into anything. They're only half-committed at best, and they are unsure whether to go after something or not. This is often the result of a lack of clarity (i.e., they don't know what they want and/or why they want it). As a result, they pursue something for the wrong reasons (e.g., to look cool, make money or generate attention). However, because this goal isn't really important to them, they procrastinate and, sooner or later, give up.

On the other hand, when what you want is truly aligned with your values and purpose, you'll feel motivated and will be able to stick to your goals for months, years or even decades.

Therefore, you need to spend time identifying what you want and avoid setting half-baked goals just because you doubt your ability to reach your real ones. Such thinking will not generate a powerful enough desire for you to strive to reach them. On top of which, these goals won't even be the ones you genuinely want in the first place.

The whole point of setting goals is to start you on an exciting journey that will enable you to grow into a better person. It is to give you an opportunity to express yourself, broadcast your values and make your personality shine. In other words, your goals create the necessary conditions for the expression of your true self.

So why not go after what you *really* want? You may or may not make it, but you will have much more energy and the journey will be much more exciting. As the entrepreneur, Jim Rohn, said, *"You want to set a goal that is big enough that in the process of achieving it you become someone worth becoming."*

So, what do you truly desire? Why is the ideal you envision so important? What could you do to strengthen your aspiration further and turn it into a burning desire that will move you closer to your goals?

1. Creating a burning desire

A thought without desire has no power, it is merely a fleeting whim, a wish, an indistinguishable noise in the background of your consciousness. Meanwhile, a thought that is believed, cherished, and given the gift of attention can generate the conditions for its manifestation in the real world. This is why, to become reality, a thought must be energized with desire, sustained over the long term and acted upon for as long as necessary.

For instance, I had a burning desire to write about personal development and make a living from it. So, I kept thinking about that goal, I read books on the topic and I felt compelled to begin writing. Then, I maintained that desire long term and kept writing week after week, month after month until I achieved tangible results. When I was a salaried employee, I wrote in the morning, at lunchtime, in the evenings, and on weekends. During working hours, I kept thinking I should be writing instead of sitting at my desk, wondering what I was doing there. The desire to spend more time writing consumed me to the point where I needed to do something about it. Eventually, I quit my job to focus on writing full time.

Now, I'm not telling you to quit your job tomorrow to pursue your passion. I simply want to give you an illustration of how desire works and how it will generate results over the long term, provided you cultivate a burning desire, sustain it for long enough and act on it repeatedly.

2. Emotionalizing your goals

For your thoughts to have power and for your goals to be attained, you must emotionalize them. How? By stacking all the reasons you want to reach these goals. For instance, perhaps you want to pursue a specific career, build a family, contribute to a cause or become financially independent, but why? Why are these things important to you?

Goals without a strong enough "why" are merely wishes, and wishes don't penetrate your consciousness deeply enough to drive concrete actions that will yield results. Thoughts you fail to nourish with the power of concentration and the energy of desire will never become powerful enough to create anything significant in the real world. Think about it this way:

How could anything intangible like a thought ever manifest in the real world without being "solidified" by intense desire and determined focus sustained over time?

For example, you won't find yourself on an exotic beach enjoying your life as an early retiree just because you had that thought once. Similarly, you won't land your ideal job just because you dreamed about it one night. It's only by obsessing over a thought that you will feel compelled to take action for long enough to achieve the corresponding results.

Now I'd like you to think of something you want to make happen in your life. It could be finding your dream job, meeting the right person or becoming financially independent. Why is this goal so important to you? Why must you *absolutely* reach it? The more reasons you have, the better. When coming up with your "whys" make sure they are:

- Specific (i.e., you can explain them in great detail), and
- Emotionalized (i.e., they are linked to your core values, purpose or passion).

Let's say one of your goals is to make more money. If so, why? What will money do for you? Below are examples of reasons why making money might be important to you:

- Being able to buy healthier and more expensive food (health),
- Buying a home closer to your parents (family values),
- Investing in a passion project (passion),
- Providing your children with a great education (family values),

- Being able to retire early and do what you love (freedom/passion), and
- Traveling and taking longer vacations (freedom/passion).

Next to each benefit, I've added the value it may relate to. This is because your "why" will only be strong when it is linked with core values you care deeply about. For example, if freedom is something to which you aspire beyond anything else, you might find it relatively easy to motivate yourself to make more money and save it diligently so that you can retire early and have more time to do things you love.

Consequently, make sure that your "why" is connected to your core values, because this will help you create an intense desire to reach your goals or vision.

3. Further energizing your goals

The next step is to energize your goals further by making all the reasons they must come true even more specific. For each benefit you identified previously, answer the questions below:

1) What exactly would this look like?

2) Why does this matter?

Try to answer each question in as much detail as possible. The more specific you are, the more emotional fuel you'll receive. Let's look at some benefits we identified previously:

- Being able to buy healthier and more expensive food (health) —> What type of food will you buy exactly? What will your breakfast, lunch and dinner look like? And why does it matter to you?
- Buying a home closer to your parents (family values) —> What will your house look like? How big will it be? How close to your parents' home will it be? And why does it matter to you?
- Investing in a passion project (passion) —> What kind of

passion project? How much time will you spend on it? And why does it matter?

The more clarity you generate, the more you'll be able to energize your goals. As you stack all the benefits together and think of them often, you'll find yourself much more motivated to work toward your goals and turn your thoughts and dreams into reality.

* * *

Action step

Complete the exercise using your action guide:

- Write down a few things you really desire.
- Among these things, select the one that excites you the most.
- Then, write down all the benefits you'll gain from achieving that goal.
- Finally, for each benefit, write down what exactly it would look like and why it matters.

12

WILLINGNESS TO FACE DISCOMFORT

How often do you move beyond your comfort zone and do something that actually scares you?

We all have our own model of reality. This model determines what we think is and isn't possible for us. You may find yourself saying things such as, "I'm not the type of person who does X, Y, Z". But is this really true? Perhaps you're not as gifted as other people in a given area, but you can always improve. With enough practice, you could excel at almost anything. You might even discover unsuspected talents.

The limitations you impose on yourself reduce your field of possibilities. The most effective way to overcome your self-imposed limitations is to move beyond your comfort zone often. By doing something you perceive as uncomfortable or even impossible, you can create a major shift in your thinking and open yourself up to a whole new world of possibility.

So, when was the last time you did something you considered "impossible"? And how did you feel as a result?

I've noticed that whenever I try something scary, I experience a sense of relief. I feel good about myself and proud to have challenged myself. I believe these positive feelings are signs the universe sends us to remind us of our true nature and our almost unlimited potential. It's a reward we get for moving toward the truth that most of our limitations exist only in our mind. And the only way to generate that reward is to take action and do what we thought impossible for us.

The bottom line is, you must be willing to face discomfort in order to further utilize the power of belief. Remember that believing is inevitable. When you do certain things, you will inevitably develop your ability to believe. Moving beyond your comfort zone is one of these things.

1. How to face discomfort

Now, you might wonder what you can do to start facing discomfort and move beyond your comfort zone. After all, it requires courage and is far from easy to do.

In his classic book, *The Magic of Thinking Big*, David J. Schwartz presents a simple formula to overcome fear which can be summed up in three words, "action cures fears". As this concept suggests, immediate action destroys fear at its roots before it spreads and invades our minds.

Years ago, I went bungee jumping with a couple of friends. We were about to jump from a sixty-seven-meter-high bridge above a river and, when my turn came, I knew that I had to jump right away. If I had hesitated and looked down at the river, fear would have kicked in and I would probably never have jumped. So, when I was told to go, I jumped immediately.

The same happens in our daily life. When we hesitate, we give fear the opportunity to invade our minds. Immediate action will stop our minds generating endless rationalizations and inflated stories that aren't grounded in reality.

A key point to understand is that our brain's primary function is to ensure our survival. This survival instinct tends to prevent us from doing anything new or scary. It is our brain's way to avoid wasting energy and enhance our odds of survival. In short, our brains use rationalization and fear to prevent us from doing anything it perceives as a threat. Even in today's world, where most of us rarely face real physical threats to our survival, our mind interprets things like the risk of rejection and the exposure to new experiences as potential dangers, making us more and more risk averse.

Below are a few practical tips to help you move beyond your comfort zone.

a. Starting small

Moving out of your comfort zone doesn't mean doing something that scares you to death. You can gradually ease away from your comfort zone by taking small steps. For instance, I'm an introvert and I'm rather uncomfortable putting myself out there. These days, I'm sometimes interviewed on podcasts. A few years ago, this sort of thing would have terrified me, but now I find it not too big of a deal (though it can still be a little uncomfortable). This is because I've already pushed myself beyond my comfort zone in the past by recording YouTube videos. The more videos I recorded, the more accustomed I grew to the process. My next uncomfortable thing was doing Facebook Live. Again, the more experience I gained, the less scary it became. If I hadn't done these things before, being interviewed would have been a far more uncomfortable experience.

The point is, whatever your comfort zone is right now, you can dramatically expand it way beyond your imagination. In a few years from now, you could very well be doing things you would have thought out of the question today. This is a real possibility. Remember, the walls defining your comfort zone are purely created by your imagination.

b. Doing the impossible

Right now, what is the most impossible thing for you to do? Is it making a speech in front of a large audience? Leading a team? Asking for a promotion? Cold calling a prospect?

Whatever it may be, let me tell you this: it is absolutely possible for you to overcome this fear!

So, what if you could do the impossible? What if you could accomplish something this week that you had always considered impossible (for you)?

Doing something way beyond your current level of comfort can dramatically expand your comfort zone, and it can do so in a short period of time. Once completed, you will suddenly realize how much more you're capable of achieving. You may even start thinking, "What else can I do?"

This will create a whole new dynamic in your life.

c. Getting support

Sometimes, finding the courage to take action on your own can be difficult, and doing the impossible might be a little too overwhelming (for now).

Years after my bungee jumping experience, I went skydiving. This time it was different. I didn't have to make the jump alone. The expert I was tethered to did all the real work. Having someone to help me jump made things significantly easier. The point I'm making is, sometimes you need support to help you move beyond your comfort zone and unlock your potential.

Other people can help you grow by:

Being a role model. Comfort zones vary from one person to another. When you surround yourself with people whose comfort zone is larger than yours, you will start perceiving your fears and limitations differently. For instance, you'll be more likely to overcome your shyness if you share a house with outgoing people. This is because they are likely to put you in uncomfortable situations you would normally avoid. Additionally, as you watch them interact with other people confidently, you'll start shifting your perspective into believing you can do the same thing. If you're willing to overcome your shyness, such an environment will help you tremendously.

Holding you accountable. It's easier to take action and do things that scare you when someone such as a coach holds you accountable. Having an accountability partner can also be effective, providing you are both fully committed and willing to call each other out (in a gentle and supportive way).

Encouraging you to take action. People can also offer encouragement. Support from family and friends can be extremely powerful. As we've seen previously, designing an empowering environment is critical if you are to build confidence and achieve more success in life.

* * *

Action step

Complete the exercise below using your action guide:

- Select one thing you believe is impossible (or very challenging) for you.
- Think of the smallest step you could take in that direction and write it down.

Alternatively, if you can muster the courage, do that one impossible thing right now.

The power of belief is one of your biggest assets. Ensure you make the most of it by building an empowering environment, leveraging the power of repeated actions, developing an intense desire for your goals and moving beyond your comfort zone. As you do so, your confidence will inevitably grow. Finally, don't forget to be patient with yourself (see also **PART V.** *Sustaining belief long term, section C. Winning the emotional game*).

PART V

SUSTAINING BELIEF LONG TERM

Believe in yourself! Have faith in your abilities! Without a humble but reasonable confidence in your own powers you cannot be successful or happy.

— NORMAN VINCENT PEALE, MINISTER AND AUTHOR.

You can only unleash the true power of belief when you are able to sustain a high level of belief over a long period of time. True belief is not simply about telling people how you're going to crush your goals, how successful you're going to be or how you will win the competition you're excited about. Although talking positively about your goal is important, it is not enough. Many people are excited when they start a new venture. They may work on it all day long for weeks, but then they encounter setbacks. And with each new setback, their self-esteem takes a hit. They begin to doubt themselves. They start to think that they're not smart enough, not good enough, or perhaps something is inherently wrong with them. As a result, they lose faith. They begin to work less and less. Their initial enthusiasm wears off and they end up giving up on that goal. Then, they repeat that process over and over with subsequent goals. Eventually, they may reach the point where they stop believing in themselves and stop setting goals at all.

Does this seem familiar? If so, don't worry. We'll see how you can change that in this section.

The point is, your true power lies in your ability to keep believing for months or years, regardless of your external situation. When you're able to sustain belief long term, you can achieve almost anything you desire. And you can certainly surprise yourself by accomplishing things you would never have thought possible. This is the power of long-term belief.

13

THE POWER OF LONG-TERM THINKING

The ability to think long term, and as often as possible, is one of the best predictors of success. As the saying goes, we overestimate what we can accomplish in one year while underestimating what we can accomplish in ten. Sure, your dreams may seem unattainable, but what if you take the first step and keep moving forward at your own pace for the next decade? Who knows where you could end up?

When I was eighteen, I didn't know I would begin to study Japanese. Less than five years later, I found myself attending economics, politics and philosophy classes in a Japanese university—and all the classes were in Japanese. Similarly, less than five years ago, I didn't know I would become a writer. Today, I've written over twenty books and have sold more than 100,000 copies.

And who knows what I will be doing in another five years.

The point I'm making is that, if you approach your goals with a long-term viewpoint, you'll often find yourself accomplishing far more than you had originally imagined. Thinking in the longer term will enable you to alleviate your doubts. You will know that as long as you keep going and improving, you'll most likely reach your goals or, at least, make significant progress toward them. This is why adopting a long-term perspective is so powerful and important.

I'm not the most confident person in the world, but I do excel at remaining patient and persevering until I reach my goals. And the reason I can do this is thanks to the foundational beliefs I developed over time such as, "I can always improve", "If others can, I can" and, "If I can do it once, I can do it again". These beliefs drive my actions and allow me to eliminate my former fears and doubts. They act like guiding stars pointing toward long-term success. They've become the programming that enables my software (my mind) to operate at its best.

As you integrate these core beliefs, you will start feeling and acting differently. You will persevere where others give up. You will aim to improve while others become complacent. As you do so, you will inevitably become a better and more confident version of yourself.

In my experience, long-term thinkers tend to be healthier, happier and more successful than other people. But long-term thinking doesn't come naturally. If anything, we're wired to think short term. Our ancestors didn't have the luxury of thinking years into the future —they were too busy trying to find their next meal and survive.

Nowadays, with little or no immediate physical threats and plenty of food available (for most of us), it should be theoretically easier to think long term. Yet, we still struggle to do so. This is not surprising, considering our attention has now become a valuable resource everyone is vying for. For example:

- Facebook spends millions to find ways to "hijack" our brains and make us addicted to their platform,
- Developers create apps encouraging instant gratification by using notifications, pop-ups and other tricks, and
- Marketers promise us quick results, playing on our natural need for immediate gratification instead of encouraging us to think long term.

Most successful people aren't addicted to social media nor do they look for get-rich-quick schemes. Instead, they patiently create their future one step at a time by taking consistent action to move toward their vision. They build solid foundations week after week, month after month, year after year, knowing that playing the long-term game will eventually pay dividends.

Once you understand the power of long-term thinking, you'll begin to cherish your vision. Each day, you'll advance your pieces on the chessboard. Knowing that life is a marathon, you'll pace yourself to ensure you'll cross the finish line.

For instance, while many authors put a couple of books out and give up in the absence of positive results, I paced myself, writing and publishing books consistently month after month. In short, while other writers were sprinting, I was running a marathon—and I was firmly committed to finishing the race.

Remember, there is no such thing as overnight success. People who achieve great success in any area have spent years working on their craft, whether in public or in private. Therefore, I encourage you to let go of short-termism and adopt long-term thinking instead. Believe that by thinking long term you can achieve almost anything you desire.

1. Long-term belief vs. temporary self-doubt

Using the power of belief to transform any area of your life doesn't require you to remove self-doubt completely. In fact, people who never doubt themselves tend to be deluded and will, in most cases, never achieve their biggest goals.

As you work toward your goals, you will inevitably experience self-doubt. You will not always be as confident as you'd like to be. You may procrastinate. You may want to escape. You may feel as though you can't succeed. And that's okay. What truly matters is that you never lose sight of the big picture and understand that you can (and will) become better over the long term.

- You might not be a good speaker right now, but what about

in a couple of years? How great will you become if you keep working on your craft consistently for two years?

- You might not sell many copies of your first book, but what will happen if you keep writing for five years, releasing several books a year, and improving your craft in the process?
- You might not be good at cooking, but what if you attend cooking classes and practice at home several times a week for six months?

In short, when in doubt, shift your focus to the long-term picture. Practice thinking in terms of years or decades, rather than days or weeks.

For example, when I started writing books and articles, I had a long-term vision. I understood that if I remained consistent, learned as much as I could and never gave up, I would eventually improve and would have a good shot at becoming a full-time writer.

Over time, I kept cultivating my ability to think in the long term. I stopped expecting one book or article to go viral. I abandoned the idea that some event would magically make me an instant success. Instead, I started believing in the process, knowing that, in the end, something would work out and make me an "overnight success".

The point is, I did experience self-doubt. But I was also confident in my ability to improve over time. So, although my first few books didn't sell well, I kept writing. Eventually, I started seeing some success. My seventh book took off and my ninth book was an even bigger hit with tens of thousands of copies sold to date.

Did I get lucky? Probably. But I provoked my luck. I kept writing books in a market with high demand, grew my fanbase, collaborated with more authors, and I ran more ads. I did everything in my power to reach my goal of making a living through my writing.

The bottom line is, the more you can eliminate self-doubt and build unshakeable belief, the better. However, removing self-doubt completely is unrealistic. It is more important to ensure you integrate the core belief that you can and will improve over the long term.

People who achieve success in their chosen field are not necessarily the most talented ones, but they are often the most patient and the most consistent. For instance, they are:

- The YouTuber who's been creating one video a week for five years—not the one who shoots one video a day just to give up three months later,
- The entrepreneur who's been working on his or her side hustle twenty hours a week for five or ten years—not the one who works eighty hours a week only to burn out after a few months, and
- The musician who keeps playing his or her instrument several times a week for years—not the one who gives up as soon as it becomes too difficult.

True belief is about being absolutely convinced of your ability to improve over the long term. It's knowing you are resourceful enough to figure it out. It's understanding that if others can, you can, too. Therefore, when self-doubt creeps in, don't panic. Remind yourself that you have time. Have faith in your ability to improve and keep going. As you do so, you'll cultivate a stronger sense of self-belief over time.

* * *

Action step

Answer the following questions using your action guide:

- If you were a long-term thinker, what would you start doing differently?
- Think of one goal you failed to achieve in the past. Now, if you could go back in time and use the power of long-term belief, what would you do differently?

2. The power of determination

> The hundreds of super successful people I have interviewed for this and other books, almost every one of them told me, 'I was not the most gifted or talented person in my field, but I chose to believe anything was possible. I studied, practiced, and worked harder than the others, and that's how I got where I am'.

— JACK CANFIELD, AUTHOR AND MOTIVATIONAL SPEAKER.

Believing you can improve comes with a great benefit—it enables you to persevere more than almost anybody else. My experience has led me to believe that perseverance is one of the keys to achieving anything worthwhile in life. In most cases, if you keep going, try one more time, improve your skills, fine-tune your strategy, or ask for help, you'll eventually obtain the results you want.

But to develop grit, you must adopt the belief that you can figure things out, and that, even though you might not be good enough yet, you can and will improve. Again, grit is not about eliminating self-doubt completely, it's about having enough faith in your capabilities to keep going until you hit your target. It is said that Thomas Edison tried 10,000 different types of filaments before he could create a light bulb that finally worked. 10,000! Can you imagine having such perseverance? Can you imagine being able to try things over and over until you found something that works? Think of what you could accomplish with such a level of determination.

The truth is that any goal worth pursuing will require a lot of time and a great deal of effort. And that's how it should be. Consequently, rather than complaining, learn to enjoy the process leading to the achievement of your goals. Cultivate grit. Make it part of your identity. Take pride in being the persistent person you are.

In addition to the foundational beliefs that I introduced in **Part IV**, let me introduce one more core belief that will help you develop grit:

"Others will give up; therefore, I will succeed."

Few people use the power of perseverance. Most give up too soon. Here is something to realize. When you feel like throwing in the towel, so do others—and most of them will. Now, the key question is, if you plan on giving up when everybody else does, why did you even start in the first place?

True perseverance happens when you have all the reasons to give up, but don't. It is when you can wake up each day and start again with unaltered enthusiasm regardless of yesterday's failures. It is when you choose to reconnect with your initial "why" and push a little harder and try one more time.

When you use the power of perseverance, your so-called competition disappears. Why? Because most people give up as soon as they face their first major setback. But *you* are different. You use the power of belief to keep going far longer than the average person ever will.

The bottom line is, when you're firmly committed to achieving your goal, you immediately eliminate the majority of your competition.

For instance, while there are hundreds of thousands of aspiring writers, only a fraction will earn a living from their craft. But if you think long term, build confidence and develop real determination, you have a great shot at becoming a full-time writer. First, most writers will give up within twelve months when they fail to see any tangible results. Second, among those who will continue, few will have the mindset and confidence required to succeed. Therefore, if you keep writing consistently and for long enough, your odds of making a living from your writing improve all the time.

You can apply the same logic for pretty much any goal you choose to pursue.

a. Developing grit

While some people may be naturally more resilient than others, grit, like most things, is a skill that can be developed over time. The success expert, Brian Tracy, defines grit as the number one quality of a successful person. In one of his interviews he said the following:

"The most important quality you can have is to be unstoppable, is to make a decision in advance that you will never give up. You don't make a decision when you have the setback or the disappointment, when you are down. You make it in advance."

Then, he added:

"If you want to become unstoppable, whenever you feel any kind of a disappointment, you just say, 'Wait a minute. I am unstoppable! I never quit. I never quit.' And pretty soon it's programmed in. Write it down, 'I am unstoppable. I am unstoppable', like your teacher used to make you write it down fifty times. I am unstoppable. And what happens is, it locks into your subconscious mind and you're prepared, so that when you have the inevitable disappointments and setbacks, you just bounce back."

What he said resonated with me as I used a similar method to develop grit. Over the past couple of years, I've been repeating to myself sentences such as:

- I am the most persistent person I ever met,
- Quitting is not an option. It's not in my vocabulary,
- I never stop,
- There is no event, person or circumstance in the world that can stop me from achieving my goals,
- I never give up. It's just who I am, and
- Even if the entire world was against me, I would keep going.

By talking to myself that way, over and over again, I created a new identity—the identity of a person who refuses to quit. I decided beforehand that no matter how many setbacks I encountered along the way, I would keep going. I wouldn't let anything prevent me from achieving my goals.

I would *not* quit!

You can do the same. You can choose to see yourself as an extremely resilient person who never quits. And as you practice persevering in moments where you would previously have given up, you'll strengthen that identity.

Becoming unstoppable is a choice. So, decide today that quitting is not something you do. Then, see how things change for you in the coming months and years.

b. Two powerful tips to develop grit

Now, let's look at two practical tips you can use to develop more grit.

1) Envision the worst-case scenario

There are a few things you can do to develop grit. The first is to imagine what could go wrong. By envisioning the worst-case scenario ahead of time, you will be able to deal with setbacks better. Remember that to become "unstoppable", you need to make a decision beforehand that you will never give up. And knowing exactly what could make you give up definitely helps.

For instance, when I started self-publishing, I envisioned what the worst-case scenarios would look like. Some of these scenarios were:

* Amazon closing my account.
* Losing all my files on my computer (which did happen).
* Not making any money for years (which also happened).
* Running out of money.

I found this exercise very helpful, especially considering what happened in 2017. During that year, the computer I had been using for six years broke down. As a result, I lost all my data including two books I had finished writing (but had yet to publish).

One of my friends told me that if he had been in the same situation, he would have been devastated. However, while I certainly was not happy about it, I didn't let it affect me. Instead, I immediately resumed work and rewrote both books from scratch. If I hadn't been prepared for that eventuality, I would have been much more adversely affected.

The bottom line is, for whatever goal you're going after, take a few minutes to envision the worst-case scenario, then see yourself reacting in the best possible way. Finally, resolve not to give up.

2) Determine your threshold for giving up

Another thing you can do to build resilience is to determine exactly what events or circumstances could lead you to give up. This approach is much more effective than just saying, "I will never give up" or "I will do whatever it takes to reach my goals", because it is usually not true. So, try to come up with specific criteria for giving up. Perhaps, you can allow yourself to give up after a certain period of time. Perhaps you can throw in the towel if you run out of money. Perhaps you can quit if you fail to hit a target by a set date (number of products sold, clients acquired, et cetera).

This approach will tell you when you can give up, giving you the peace of mind needed to keep going for as long as your criteria haven't been met.

The way I used this technique is by setting what I called a "Bullet-Proof Timeframe", which is a period of time I give myself to work on a specific goal. I can abandon that particular goal if things don't work as planned, but I can never quit *before* my self-imposed deadline. For my goal of earning a living from my books, I chose a three-year timeframe (from April 2017 to April 2020). During these three years, all I needed to do was to write and publish books. Every time I felt overwhelmed or became distracted, I asked myself, "What do I need to do now?". The answer would always be, "Write more books". This method allowed me to refocus on my main goal dozens of times. As I'm writing these words, I'm nine days away from the deadline. Since April 2017, I've written sixteen books and sold over 100,000 copies. This worked out well for me.

What about you? What Bullet-Proof Timeframe will you create for yourself?

If you want to learn more about the Bullet-Proof Timeframe, refer to my book, *The One Goal*.

* * *

Action steps

Complete the following exercise using your action guide:

• Think of your major goal and then write down what the worst-case scenarios could be.
• What could make you give up on that goal? Write down the criteria that would need to be met before you throw in the towel.
• Finally, set a timeframe during which you will commit to working on that goal.

c. A story about perseverance

The following story is a wonderful illustration of the power of perseverance.

Karoly Takacs was a world-class pistol shooter. After winning major national and international competitions, he dreamed of winning an Olympic Gold Medal at the 1940 Tokyo Olympic Games.

After joining the Hungarian Army, however, his dream was crushed. While in training, a faulty grenade exploded, resulting in severe injury to his right hand, which meant he had no hopes of making it to the Olympics, let alone winning anything.

When he showed up at the 1939 Hungarian National Pistol Shooting Championship, his colleagues were delighted to see him, complimented his courage and thanked him for his willingness to come and cheer for them. You can imagine their surprise when he said he wasn't there to cheer for them, but to compete with them.

But what is even more surprising is that he didn't just compete, he won the competition! Sounds impossible, right? How could he do that without the use of his right hand? The answer is simple: he used his left hand instead.

Despite the severe depression his accident caused, he managed to pull himself together. Instead of focusing on his loss, he chose to focus on what he still had—an exceptional mindset and a healthy left hand. Then, he practiced relentlessly for a year without telling anyone.

Takacs pressed on, held onto his dream and looked forward to the 1940 Olympics. Unfortunately, the 1940 Olympics were canceled due to World War II. He pushed through his disappointment and began practicing for the 1944 Olympics. But they were canceled, too.

He continued training anyway and, in 1944, finally qualified for the 1948 London Olympics. He ultimately won a gold medal at age thirty-eight and set a new world record in pistol shooting. Four years later, he won the gold medal yet again at the 1952 Helsinki Olympics.

As this incredible story shows, being obsessed with a goal and persevering no matter what can lead to extraordinary results. To do this, we must develop an exceptional mindset and possess enough passion to push past great obstacles.

If you want more inspirational stories like this one, you can refer to my planner, *The Ultimate Goal Setting Planner: Become an Unstoppable Goal Achiever in 90 Days or Less*. In it, I share twelve great stories that will inspire you to go after your wildest goals.

14

HOW TO TRANSITION FROM SHORT-TERM TO LONG-TERM THINKING

While some people may be better than others at it, thinking long term is a skill everyone can acquire. In this section, we'll discuss seven specific things you can do to develop that skill. These are:

1. Creating a long-term vision.
2. Thinking of your long-term goals often.
3. Carving out time to focus on the big picture.
4. Learning to love the process.
5. Letting go of the fear of missing out.
6. Reminding yourself to be patient.
7. Focusing on all the reasons you can be successful.

1. Creating a long-term vision

The first step to become more future-oriented is to create a long-term vision. It is difficult, if not impossible, to think in the long term unless you have a vision to move toward. Without a clear vision, you risk wasting time performing tasks that are out of alignment with your goals. You need to make sure that the tasks you work on today move you closer to your ultimate vision.

Action step

Think of a long-term goal or vision and write it down in your action guide.

2. Thinking of your long-term goals often

Once you have established a long-term goal, you want to look at it on a regular basis. You can do so by:

- Creating a vision board and placing it somewhere you'll see it often,
- Writing down your long-term goal on a sheet of paper and hanging it on your desk or somewhere you can see it daily, and/or
- Reading your long-term goal every day/week.

The more often you think about your long-term goals, the more focus-oriented you will become.

Action step

Using your action guide, write your long-term goal/vision and put it somewhere you can see it easily and often.

3. Carving out time to focus on the big picture

To stay focused on your long-term vision, I invite you to dedicate time during your week to zoom out and focus on the bigger picture. For instance, you could spend thirty-to-sixty minutes on Sundays to assess your progress and make sure you're moving in the right direction. During this time, ask yourself the following questions:

- What am I satisfied with?
- What do I need to improve?
- What could I do differently to accelerate my progress?
- If I could start the week again, what would I do differently?
- If I keep doing what I've done this week, will I achieve my long-term goal? If not, what do I need to change?
- Is my current strategy the best one? If not, what should I change to improve it?
- What actions create most of my results? What could I do to spend more time on these specific activities?
- What tasks didn't generate good results? Could I get rid of some of them?
- If I could only work on one major goal or project this week/month/year, what would it be and why?

Having weekly strategic sessions will ensure you carve out time to consider your future and help you become an effective long-term thinker.

* * *

Action step

Schedule time every week to focus on the big picture. Go through the list of questions above to help you do so. (You'll also find them in your action guide.)

4. Learning to love the process

The power of belief is only truly effective when it is sustained over the long term. Short bursts of confidence or brief phases of excitement will never enable you to achieve your most ambitious goals. Since worthy goals require time and effort, the best way to reach them is to design an effective process you'll stick to long term. In short, you need to fall in love with the process.

You might buy into the myth that one specific goal, when attained, will finally make you happy. However, this is not how your brain works. In truth, you're at your happiest when pursuing meaningful goals. This is why as soon as you reach a goal, you can't help setting a new one. This means that most of your happiness occurs during the process leading to the achievement of your goals. As such, obsessing over the results is missing the point. The joy you experience after reaching your goal will only be short-lived. The process *is* the real goal to focus on. As such, the best way to be fulfilled is to enjoy the process leading to the attainment of worthy goals.

Learn to love the process and don't forget to celebrate each milestone reached along the way. This is the best way to build your confidence while using the power of long-term thinking.

* * *

Action step

Complete the sentence below using your action guide:

For me, focusing more on the process would mean ...

5. Letting go of the fear of missing out

Many people are afraid of missing out on life. They live in fear of missing that one person, event or opportunity. For instance:

- When they can't attend a party, they become anxious. What if something amazing happens and they aren't there to see it?
- When they travel, they try to see as many monuments and places as possible, packing their days with numerous visits. They usually spend hours researching for fear of missing the one thing they must absolutely see.
- When they're unable to date someone they like, some people feel discouraged, wondering if they will ever meet such a wonderful person again.

Ultimately, the fear of missing out comes from a "scarcity mindset". It results from a lack of trust in the world and in its ability to provide more opportunities than you can imagine. Perhaps, more importantly, it is the manifestation of a lack of trust in yourself and in your capacity to create wonderful memories. In reality, there is no shortage of pleasant experiences for you to enjoy. There is no limit to the number of great memories you can create.

The problem when you fear missing out, is that you tend to be easily distracted by new opportunities. This is why you must learn to control that fear better. People who fall for the "Shiny Object Syndrome" are a good illustration. These individuals believe there is a magic pill "out there somewhere", and they can't stop themselves from looking for it.

On the other hand, long-term thinkers understand this is an inaccurate way of looking at the world. They know they need to establish a sound strategy, refine it regularly over time and stick to it for the long term. To succeed, they know they will have to "miss out" on many things before they reach their goal.

By being too scared of missing out on parties, events or opportunities, you risk missing out on your life. In short, you risk selling out your long-term potential for short-term gratification.

* * *

Action step

Complete the exercises below using your action guide:

- Write down the area(s) of your life in which you experience fear of missing out.
- Select one specific area or goal and write down all the opportunities that actually exist out there. What are your options? What could you do about it?
- Take a moment to appreciate all the opportunities available to you.

6. Reminding yourself to be patient

For most people, being a long-term thinker doesn't come naturally. To improve your ability to think long term, you must remind yourself of the importance of remaining patient.

While people think I'm naturally patient, I'm not. I want things to happen now. But at the same time, I appreciate the value of patience. I understand that any meaningful goal requires months or years of work and that with enough patience, I can achieve almost anything I want. I understand that by using the power of belief for an extensive period of time, I will most likely achieve wonderful things in the long run.

* * *

Action step

Regularly remind yourself that you have time. To do this, you can:

- Create your own mantras such as "life is a marathon, not a sprint", or simply "be patient", and think of them often, write them down and/or display them on your desk, or on your wall,
- Watch Gary Vee's YouTube videos, *Overnight success* and *People have forgotten the art of patience*,
- Visualize everything you've already done in the past few months/years and remind yourself of how much more time you have to achieve even greater things, and
- Remember that the thoughts you keep focusing on using the power of belief will, over time, create the corresponding results—provided you're acting on them consistently enough and for long enough.

7. Focusing on all the reasons you can be successful

Long-term thinking involves focusing on all the long-term opportunities waiting for you. It requires you to put your energy into all the reasons you can achieve your long-term projects. By developing the habit of focusing on everything you can do to move closer to your goals, you will cultivate a more positive mindset that will help you remain optimistic. In short, we can say that by doing so, you leverage your power of belief by projecting it into the future (i.e., focusing on possibilities). The more you focus on what you can do moving forward, the better you'll feel and the more action you'll take to close the gap between where you are and where you want to be.

* * *

Action step

Using your action guide, write down all the reasons you can be successful. Repeat the same exercise whenever necessary.

By practicing all the exercises above, you'll find yourself thinking of the long-term picture much more often than you used to. As you do so, you will make better decisions, you will put in place more effective processes and you will make more consistent progress toward your goals. Finally, you will significantly boost your long-term confidence.

15

WINNING THE EMOTIONAL GAME

Your ability to sustain a high level of belief in yourself and in your goals is critical. However, the truth is that you are bound to have ups and downs. One day you might feel at the top of the world, while the next day you might feel like giving up. This is why it's essential you learn how to control your emotions better. Once you understand what emotions are, how they work and how to manage them better, you'll be able to develop strong emotional resilience. This will help you to overcome self-doubt and keep moving toward your goals when things don't go as planned.

The good news is that you *can* learn to control your emotions better. We'll see how in this section.

1. How your emotions distort your thinking

Your emotions distort your thinking and directly impact your behavior. For instance, when you feel good, you're more creative and have more energy to act toward your goals. Conversely, when you're feeling sad or depressed, your motivation will fall, and you will invite in more and more negative thinking. In this negative condition, everything will seem gloomy and you'll be unable to think clearly or act in a constructive way. Therefore, to use the power of belief to your advantage, you must learn to understand your emotions better. You must become their master, not their slave.

Below are three characteristics of negative emotions you need to be aware of:

a. Negative emotions cast a spell

When you're under the influence of negative emotions, it might seem impossible to break free from them. You may feel the urge to focus on the same disempowering thoughts repeatedly.

For instance, this is the case when you have an argument with a loved one or a friend and can't stop playing the scene in your mind over and over again.

b. Negative emotions filter your experiences

Negative emotions act as a filter that taints the quality of your experiences. During a negative episode, you can perceive every experience through this filter. Although the world outside may remain the same, you will experience it in a completely different way, based on the way you feel at the time.

For instance, when you're sad, you might not enjoy the food you eat, the movie you watch or the activities in which you engage. You only see the negative side of things and end up feeling trapped and powerless. On the other hand, when you're in a positive mood, everything in life appears better. Food tastes great, you're naturally friendlier and you enjoy all the activities you partake in.

c. Negative emotions attract more negative emotions

When you're in a negative emotional state, you'll begin to attract more emotions on a similar "wave" (i.e., more negative emotions).

For instance, you might be in a bad mood because your boss yelled at you at work. This may lead you to think about some issues you have with your partner. You may then remember your back pain and start obsessing over it. As a result, you will feel even worse.

2. Four tips to help you overcome emotional traps

By now, you understand that your emotions can distort your thinking, negatively impact your behavior and erode your self-confidence. If you don't keep them under control, they will wreak havoc in your life. To manage your emotions more effectively, I encourage you to do the following:

Tip #1—Recognize the idea that you are not your emotions. Your emotions can never define you. For instance, being sad for months doesn't make you a lesser person than you were before, during times when you were happy. Emotions are like clouds hiding the sun. The sun is *always* there. You are the sun. Sure, your emotions can trick you beyond anything you can imagine—and they will—but they *cannot* attack your essence.

Tip #2—Don't cluster negative emotions together. Negative emotions attract more negative emotions. Therefore, start noticing whenever you are clustering issues together (e.g., having back pain, hating your job and being in the middle of an argument with your partner). Then, look at each issue separately. By doing so, you will realize that, when taken independently, these issues might not be as big a challenge as you thought, or they are at least more manageable. In short, don't stack negative thoughts together. Instead, compartmentalize them, and deal with them individually.

Tip #3—Avoid making important decisions when under the spell of strong emotions. Your emotions distort your thinking. This goes for both negative *and* positive emotions. Consequently, avoid making major decisions when you're experiencing highs (feeling hopeful, content, ecstatic, et cetera.) or lows (feeling depressed, hopeless, angry, et cetera). Instead, wait until you revert to a more neutral emotional state. In this condition you will think much more clearly and will make better decisions as a result. For example:

- Don't decide to give up on your dreams when you feel depressed. Wait until you feel better before making such an important decision.

- Don't reply to an email that makes you angry immediately. Instead, wait at least twenty-four hours.
- Don't make any promises or major decisions just after receiving great news (e.g., winning the lottery).

If you avoid making any serious decisions when under the spell of strong emotions, it will likely save you a great deal of trouble.

Tip #4—Cultivate self-compassion. How often do you make yourself miserable by figuratively beating yourself up? The worst time to do so is when you already feel bad. This is why I like to adopt what I call the "I'll beat myself up later" policy. In other words, I give myself permission to be hard on myself later, but *not* when I'm in a negative emotional state. Instead, I show myself some much-needed compassion. I encourage you to do the same thing.

Use the tips above to help you manage your emotions better and you'll be able to make better life decisions.

To learn in more detail how to manage your emotions, refer to my book, *Master Your Emotions.*

* * *

Action step

Complete the following exercises and add them to your action guide:

- Remember a time when everything felt hopeless or gloomy and you didn't believe you could be happy again. Then, realize your negative emotions eventually faded away.
- Think of three current challenges in your life one after the other. How does each make you feel? Now, visualize three things you're grateful for or excited about. Feel better now?
- Think of one poor decision you made as a result of negative emotions (anger, hopelessness, frustration) or positive emotions (joy, euphoria, excitement).
- For one full minute give yourself some words of

encouragement. Remind yourself that you're doing well, that you have noble intentions, and that you're proud of all the things you've accomplished so far. How does it make you feel?

3. The importance of self-compassion

When it comes to controlling your emotions, self-compassion plays a critical role. It acts as a safety net to your emotional well-being. When you're hard on yourself, you experience a great deal of emotional suffering. You shame yourself or experience guilt or frustration. Your self-confidence suffers and you feel trapped. Those lofty goals you had now seem completely out of reach.

In short, when you fail to use the power of self-compassion you make your life miserable. In the process, you leak an enormous amount of energy you could have used to improve yourself and take action to move toward your goals.

However, it doesn't have to be this way. You don't need to use the carrot and stick approach to motivate yourself. You don't need to beat yourself up every time you make a small mistake. This will not help you achieve your goals. If anything, it will prevent you from utilizing the power of belief.

The reason many of us lack self-compassion is because we never learned to talk to ourselves in a loving and caring way. We act as though we're on probation on earth. That is, we act as though a single mistake could reveal the "truth" that we aren't good enough in some way. By criticizing ourselves over and over, we hope to live up to our unrealistic standards. But this approach is counter-productive and even destructive. In the long term, acting this way won't enable us to be fulfilled or successful.

a. Three disempowering myths about self-compassion

The first step to developing greater self-compassion is to dispel some of the common myths that harm us.

Myth #1—you need to be harsh with yourself to get anything done.

The first myth is the belief that you won't get anything done unless you're harsh with yourself. But is that true? Will you become suddenly lazy if, instead of criticizing yourself, you show yourself a healthy dose of self-compassion? Will you lie on the couch all day, doing nothing but eating potato chips and watching sitcoms on TV? Maybe, but this will likely be temporary.

Talking down to yourself when you're already struggling isn't helpful. A far better strategy is to give yourself words of encouragement and to celebrate each of your accomplishments. This will help reinforce positive behaviors and encourage you to reproduce these behaviors in the future. By doing so, you're creating a track record of success.

The truth is that self-compassion is more effective than self-criticism. Self-compassion invites you to acknowledge the undeniable truth that you are a fallible human being but that, at any given time, you're trying to do the best with what you have. Being self-compassionate enables you to keep moving forward, regardless of how many setbacks you may encounter along the way. It makes you far more resilient and spares you a great deal of unnecessary emotional suffering. As a result, you'll end up accomplishing more than you would by relying on self-criticism as your primary motivational tool.

I made the shift from self-criticism to self-compassion years ago, and I never looked back. Now, am I satisfied with everything in my life? Of course not. Do I wish I could be better in some areas of my life? Yes, of course. However, I do understand that the best way to improve is to be kind to myself and keep moving forward at my own pace.

The bottom line is, cultivating self-compassion will not lead you to become complacent. Conversely, it will make you more resilient and help you achieve more with less stress. It's like having a loving coach with you 24/7 for the rest of your life. That's a pretty cool thing to have, isn't it?

Myth #2—self-compassion is for weak-minded people. This is somewhat related to the first myth. Many people believe that being self-compassionate will make them weak. Strong people are tough. They expect the best from themselves and call themselves out when they don't do what they're supposed to do, right? Yes, but this doesn't mean you have to treat yourself poorly and make yourself suffer in the process. Strong people have the emotional intelligence to respect and encourage themselves during challenging moments. This is what makes them truly unstoppable. Yes, they demand more of themselves, but they do so in a loving manner. They don't let negative emotions break them; they accept them for what they are—temporary. By doing so, they develop stronger emotional stability than the so-called tough people, and they can persevere longer while experiencing less mental suffering.

Self-compassion is not for weak-minded people. In fact, it is a sign of strength and maturity. Strong people know how to rely on it to achieve their long-term goals and dreams.

Myth #3—Self-compassion is selfish. You might find self-compassion difficult to practice because it makes you feel as though you're being selfish or arrogant. Who are you to encourage yourself, take care of yourself, or even love yourself! As such, you may experience resistance as you begin to talk and act in a more self-compassionate way.

But is self-compassion really selfish? Is giving yourself some slack forbidden? Again, this type of thinking stems from the idea that unless you're harsh on yourself, you won't get the job done, and this comes from a lack of self-love.

When you continuously criticize yourself, all you really do is make yourself miserable, which, as a side-effect, also leads you to underperform. This is why self-compassion is not selfish. If anything, it is selfless. Because when you're able to treat yourself with more love and respect, you have more energy to direct outward, toward the world around you. In addition, the more you learn to be compassionate toward yourself, the more you'll tend to become compassionate toward others.

To conclude, being self-compassionate isn't selfish. It's an important part of self-care and is essential if you want to build your self-esteem and emotional resilience.

b. How to develop self-compassion

I used to be quite harsh on myself. I would insult myself and become angry when I failed to achieve the results I expected. Also, I would compare myself to others. Seeing how poorly I appeared to be doing in many areas of my life, I felt frustrated.

However, upon reading books and through personal experience, I began to realize that beating myself up wasn't helping me. In fact, it was actually holding me back and making me feel terrible. So, I made the radical decision to stop beating myself up. From that point on, I decided to encourage myself during challenging times, because how much good could self-criticism really do when I was already feeling down?

To let go of self-criticism and cultivate self-compassion, I began to change my internal self-talk. For instance, instead of calling myself an idiot whenever I made a mistake, I would say things like:

- It's okay, I'll do better next time.
- It's not a big deal.
- I did what I could with what I had.
- What can I learn so that I'll do a better job next time?
- Nobody is perfect.

Altering my self-talk made me realize how heavily conditioned people tend to be. We have no problem criticizing ourselves, but find it challenging to encourage ourselves. How odd is that? As I used every opportunity I could to practice self-compassion, I noticed that it was a far better strategy for long-term success and happiness. Becoming more self-compassionate didn't make me complacent. On the contrary, it increased my motivation and boosted my productivity.

1) Undertaking a 7-Day Self-Compassion Challenge

An effective way to start cultivating self-compassion is to undertake a 7-Day Self-Compassion Challenge. This challenge is simple:

For the next seven days, stop beating yourself up and stop talking to yourself in a negative way. Don't insult yourself. Don't call yourself an idiot. Don't blame yourself when you make a mistake. Instead, be kind to yourself. Don't worry about the small stuff. Most of the mistakes you make are not that big of a deal and certainly not a reason to disrespect yourself. When you feel the urge to criticize yourself, pause for a second, then tell yourself that you're doing okay. Encourage yourself to do a better job or learn a lesson when possible.

To help, you can wear a rubber band around your wrist and snap it whenever you notice that you're disrespecting yourself. Keep doing the same thing for a week and see how it affects your results as well as your overall well-being. Does it make you complacent or does it make you feel better, eager to improve and keen to move forward? Run the test and check the results.

2) Changing your self-talk

As human beings, we can choose how we talk to ourselves. Remember that our self-talk determines what we do and how we feel. Happy people tend to be optimistic, focusing most of their time and energy on the opportunities in front of them. Meanwhile, unhappy people tend to be more pessimistic than most. They see the negative side of things, looking for reasons why they can't achieve their goals or make positive changes in their lives.

What about you? What conversations are you having with yourself? Do you talk to yourself respectfully or do you use harsh words and treat yourself as though you are someone you despise?

Let's run a quick experiment. Think of words you use when you beat yourself up. Now, imagine yourself using the same words to a loved one. How do you think he or she would react?

Fortunately, you can adjust your self-talk. But first, you must notice the conversation going on in your mind. Until now, you probably never paid close attention to your self-talk. For the next twenty-four hours, make yourself acutely aware of it. Monitor how you talk to yourself, then write down what you discovered.

On a scale from 1 to 10 (with one being extremely negative and ten being extremely positive), what was the content of your self-talk? Did you beat yourself up or were you encouraging? What disempowering thoughts did you have? What negative words did you use?

Now, if you had unshakeable confidence and could stop beating yourself up completely, how would you change your self-talk? What would you start telling yourself? What would you stop saying to yourself?

4. The four motivators to build sustainable motivation

To develop unshakeable confidence long term, you must also learn to develop and maintain a high level of motivation. I believe there are four types of motivators that lead us to act, which are:

1. Love,
2. Desire,
3. Pain, and
4. Ego.

Let's look at each motivator and see how you can use them to keep your motivation high long term.

a. Love

A sincere desire to contribute to the world and make a difference in people's lives will keep you pumped up as you work toward your goal. When you have a compelling vision inspired by love, you'll be fueled by this vision and the excitement you'll feel about the impact you're making. The more you act from love and from the need to give back, the easier it will be for you to stay motivated. This is the deeper "why" behind your goal.

b. Desire

Desire is different from love in that it's not about contributing to other people. Instead, it focuses on designing the life you want for yourself. It's about living life on your own terms.

Having goals that excite you will bolster your motivation significantly. You'll feel connected to your goals, to the point that reminding yourself of what you'll gain from working on it should keep you going.

For example, one of my goals is to create an online business I'm passionate about and can make a living from. A few benefits I can think of include:

- Having the freedom to travel the world while working on my business,
- Having the ability to spend more time with my family,
- Having the freedom to live in different countries and learn foreign languages,
- Having the freedom to take vacations whenever I want,
- Being able to spend more time doing what I love,
- Having the potential to earn more money by scaling up my business (which would be impossible if I worked for someone else),
- Being in a situation where I can, and must, grow consistently and become a better person, and
- Having more time to spend on my personal growth (seminars, meditation, side projects, et cetera).

These are all things that motivate me to work on my goals every single day.

See also **PART V**. *The Belief Formula, section C. Intense Desire.*

c. Pain

Nobody wants to suffer, and we spend a lot of time shying away from pain. When used intelligently, pain can be an effective tool to motivate you when you'd rather do nothing.

When I was an employee, there were many times when I didn't feel like working on my online business. After a rough workday, I'd return home exhausted, wanting to do nothing more than rest. I bet you can relate to this feeling! I handled it by focusing on the pain I'd endure if I *didn't* work on my business and I *didn't* create the life I wanted. I asked myself the following questions:

- Do I want to work a job I hate for the rest of my life?
- Do I want to be caught in rush hour every morning and evening for the next forty years?
- Do I want to have a boss telling me what to do when I already know what I want to do with my life?
- When I reach my deathbed, will I regret not having done what I know I should have?
- How much pain will I experience when I realize I didn't have the courage, determination and perseverance to follow my dreams?
- Can I accept the pain and regret of not facing my fears and failing to make a difference through my work?

The idea of spending forty years at a job I hated gave me a serious boost of motivation. Freedom is what I valued most and, being unable to enjoy the level of freedom I wanted, was excruciating.

d. Ego

Ego can also be a powerful motivator. You can use your desire to be successful, to feel loved or to prove those who didn't believe in you wrong, to your advantage. For example, you might feel a surge of motivation when you think of how proud your parents will be when you succeed. Or the thought of showing someone who doubts you what you're really made of might get you going.

However, you need to bear in mind that if you feel a constant need to rely on your ego, you might want to spend some time working on yourself. It would be a good idea to figure out why you're trying so hard to obtain the validation of others.

I've relied, and still rely, on all four types of motivation to ensure I keep going. Below are some specific examples organized by category.

- **Love:** Knowing how much impact I can have on other people's lives makes me excited to write my books.
- **Pain:** When I felt tired after work (back when I was an employee), I visualized myself staying at a job I hate for forty years, feeling the pain and regret going with it. This gave me

an extra boost of motivation that helped me work on my goals for a few hours even when I didn't feel like it.

- **Desire:** When I felt demotivated during my journey toward becoming a full-time writer, I thought of the freedom I would be able to enjoy once I achieve my goals. This made me excited and reenergized.
- **Ego:** Although I don't like to admit it, I sometimes envision myself having achieved my wildest dreams and imagine the way others admire the person I've become.

What about you? How can you use these four motivators to inspire you to chase your vision?

To learn how to build long-lasting motivation in greater depth, refer to the second book in this series, *Master Your Motivation.*

5. The importance of enjoying the process

The famous life coach, Tony Robbins, says that "progress equals happiness" and I find this to be very true. People who stop improving and who have nothing exciting to move toward tend to feel less happy than people who do.

Consequently, if you want to be happier and become more resilient so that you can achieve your goals, I invite you to focus on the process. To do so effectively, you have to shift from someone who is overly concerned about the results to someone who takes pleasure in becoming better every day, while at the same time knowing that long-term results are inevitable.

Remember that true self-belief is the ability to believe in yourself long term. It is knowing that you will figure things out while maintaining enthusiasm day in day out, regardless of your results (or lack thereof), in the short term.

You always have the ability to believe in yourself and in your vision, and you always have the ability to learn and improve. Keep believing in yourself, keep using the power of belief you were given at birth, nail the process and stick to it until you end up where you want to be.

The right process leads to the right results

The truth is that no matter how badly you want something, you can never be sure you'll obtain it within the desired timeframe. However, you *can* build an effective process and follow it diligently. Once you learn to trust the process, you can release any self-doubts, knowing that you're doing the right thing.

For example, I can't know for sure how many copies of my books I'll sell in any given year, but I can choose how many books I'll write. Therefore, part of an effective process for me is to write (almost) every day, first thing in the morning, and to release books regularly, according to my original plan.

I cannot be sure a specific book will sell, but I can study the market and choose a topic that I believe can sell well. I don't know if any particular ad will be profitable, but I can set aside some time every day/week to optimize existing ads and create new ones. I have power over all these things.

All the things I believe I must do to reach my goals have become my process. This process is something I obsess over and measure myself against regularly. It becomes what I must follow religiously, regardless of the external results (or the lack thereof).

Sure, things such as having the end in mind and visualizing your goals are important. However, once you've done this, the only thing that truly matters is sticking to your process. If you can do that, small results will accumulate over time, leading to long-term results that may often exceed your greatest expectations.

The process *is* the goal. You must take it and its underlying habits seriously. Remember, success isn't something that happens in the future, it's something you embody every day when you do the best you can with what you have. Therefore, you don't need ten years to be successful, you can be successful today by taking the actions you believe to be the right ones. And, ultimately, that's all you can do.

* * *

Action step

Complete the following exercise, using your action guide:

- Think of a major goal.
- Now, try to come up with the best process to reach it. To do so, ask yourself, what would I need to do every day to almost guarantee I achieve this goal?

CONCLUSION

I would like to congratulate you on reading this book until the end. By now you should have developed a solid understanding of what the power of belief is and how you can use it to transform your life. Remember, nobody can take away your ability to believe in yourself and in your vision; you can only neglect it or forget about it.

I hope you'll use the power of belief to develop unwavering confidence and move closer to your ideal future life. I also hope you will use it to inspire anyone to cultivate their own underutilized ability to believe.

To do so, make sure you cultivate a new identity by incorporating the foundational beliefs below:

1. I can use my thoughts to shape my reality.
2. The universe is on my side.
3. If others can, I can.
4. I can always improve.
5. If I can do it once, I can do it again.
6. I can figure things out.
7. Failure is *not* inevitable.
8. Success is inevitable.

Then, activate the power of belief by:

- Building an empowering environment that supports the future you want to create,
- Using the power of repetition until you see tangible results,
- Cultivating an intense desire until you feel compelled to act, and
- Moving beyond your comfort zone and expanding your field of possibilities by doing "impossible things".

As you learn to sustain a high level of self-belief by focusing on the long-term picture and by controlling your emotions better, you'll magnify the power of belief and achieve things you thought impossible.

So, keep believing, put time and energy into what matters the most to you and take repeated actions until you achieve positive results. And whenever you face setbacks, learn from them, refine your approach and pursue your journey with unshakeable optimism.

This is how you make the power of belief work for you.

Finally, remember that we are the only species who can use our imagination to turn the invisible into the visible. Ensure you make the most of that extraordinary power to create a better future for yourself and for people around you.

If you have any questions or would like to share your story with me, please feel free to contact me at: thibaut.meurisse@gmail.com.

I'm always happy to learn what my readers are up to.

Warm regards,

Thibaut Meurisse

What do you think?

I hope you benefit from this book. I would be very grateful if you could take a moment to leave an honest review on Amazon.

Thanks again for your support!

Thibaut

MASTER YOUR EMOTIONS (PREVIEW)

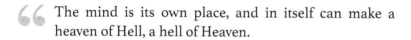 The mind is its own place, and in itself can make a heaven of Hell, a hell of Heaven.

— JOHN MILTON, POET.

We all experience a wide range of emotions throughout our lives. I had to admit, while writing this book, I experienced highs and lows myself. At first, I was filled with excitement and thrilled at the idea of providing people with a guide to help them understand their emotions. I imagined how readers' lives would improve as they learned to control their emotions. My motivation was high and I couldn't help but imagine how great the book would be.

Or so I thought.

After the initial excitement, the time came to sit down to write the actual book, and that's when the excitement wore off pretty quickly. Suddenly ideas that looked great in my mind felt dull. My writing seemed boring, and I felt as though I had nothing substantive or valuable to contribute.

Sitting at my desk and writing became more challenging each day. I started losing confidence. Who was I to write a book about emotions if I couldn't even master my own emotions? How ironic! I considered giving up. There are already plenty of books on the topic, so why add one more?

At the same time, I realized this book was a perfect opportunity to work on my emotional issues. And who doesn't suffer from negative emotions from time to time? We all have highs and lows, don't we? The key is what we *do* with our lows. Are we using our emotions to grow and learn or are we beating ourselves up over them?

So, let's talk about *your* emotions now. Let me start by asking you this:

How do you feel right now?

Knowing how you feel is the first step toward taking control of your emotions. You may have spent so much time internalizing you've lost touch with your feelings. Perhaps you answered as follows: "I feel this book could be useful," or "I really feel I could learn something from this book."

However, none of these answers reflect on how you feel. You don't 'feel like this,' or 'feel like that,' you simply 'feel.' You don't 'feel like' this book could be useful, you 'think' this book could be useful, and that generates an emotion which makes you 'feel' excited about reading it. Feelings manifest as physical sensations in your body, not as an idea in your mind. Perhaps, the reason the word 'feel' is so often overused or misused is because we don't want to talk about our emotions.

So, how do you feel now?

Why is it important to talk about emotions?

How you feel determines the quality of your life. Your emotions can make your life miserable or truly magical. That's why they are among the most essential things on which to focus. Your emotions color all your experiences. When you feel good, everything seems, feels, or tastes better. You also think better thoughts. Your energy levels are higher and possibilities seem limitless. Conversely, when you feel depressed, everything seems dull. You have little energy and you become unmotivated. You feel stuck in a place (mentally and physically) you don't want to be, and the future looks gloomy.

Your emotions can also act as a powerful guide. They can tell you something is wrong and allow you to make changes in your life. As such, they may be among the most powerful personal growth tools you have.

Sadly, neither your teachers nor your parents taught you how emotions work or how to control them. I find it ironic that just about anything comes with a how-to manual, while your mind doesn't. You've never received an instruction manual to teach you how your mind works and how to use it to better manage your emotions, have you? I haven't. In fact, until now, I doubt one even existed.

What you'll learn in this book

This book is the how-to manual your parents should have given you at birth. It's the instruction manual you should have received at school. In it, I'll share everything you need to know about emotions so you can overcome your fears and limitations and become the type of person you want to be.

More specifically, this book will help you:

- Understand what emotions are and how they impact your life
- Understand how emotions form and how you can use them for your personal growth
- Identify negative emotions that control your life and learn to overcome them
- Change your story to take better control over your life and create a more compelling future,
- Reprogram your mind to experience more positive emotions.
- Deal with negative emotions and condition your mind to create more positive ones

- Gain all the tools you need to start recognizing and controlling your emotions

Here is a more detailed summary of what you'll learn in this book:

In **Part I**, we'll discuss what emotions are. You'll learn why your brain is wired to focus on negativity and what you can do to counter this effect. You'll also discover how your beliefs impinge upon your emotions. Finally, you'll learn how negative emotions work and why they are so tricky.

In **Part II**, we'll go over the things that directly impact your emotions. You'll understand the roles your body, your thoughts, your words, or your sleep, play in your life and how you can use them to change your emotions.

In **Part III**, you'll learn how emotions form and how to condition your mind to experience more positive emotions.

And finally, in **Part IV**, we'll discuss how to use your emotions as a tool for personal growth. You'll learn why you experience emotions such as fear or depression and how they work.

Let's get started.

To start mastering your emotions today go to

mybook.to/Master_Emotions

I. What emotions are

Have you ever wondered what emotions are and what purpose they serve?

In this section, we'll discuss how your survival mechanism affects your emotions. Then, we'll explain what the 'ego' is and how it impacts your emotions. Finally, we'll discover the mechanism behind emotions and learn why it can be so hard to deal with negative ones.

Why people have a bias towards negativity

Your brain is designed for survival, which explains why you're able to read this book at this very moment. When you think about it, the probability of you being born was extremely low. For this miracle to happen, all the generations before you had to survive long enough to procreate. In their quest for survival and procreation, they must have faced death hundreds or perhaps thousands of times.

Fortunately, unlike your ancestors, you're (probably) not facing death every day. In fact, in many parts of the world, life has never been safer. Yet, your survival mechanism hasn't changed much. Your brain still scans your environment looking for potential threats.

In many ways, some parts of your brain have become obsolete. While you may not be seconds away from being eaten by a predator, your brain still gives significantly more weight to adverse events than to positive ones.

Fear of rejection is one example of a bias toward negativity. In the past, being rejected by your tribe would reduce your chances of survival significantly. Therefore, you learned to look for any sign of rejection, and this became hardwired in your brain.

Nowadays, being rejected often carries little or no consequence to your long-term survival. You can be hated by the entire world and still have a job, a roof and plenty of food on the table, yet, your brain remains programmed to perceive rejection as a threat to your survival.

This hardwiring is why rejection can be so painful. While you know most rejections are no big deal, you nevertheless feel the emotional pain. If you listen to your mind, you may even create a whole drama around it. You may believe you aren't worthy of love and dwell on a rejection for days or weeks. Worse still, you may become depressed as a result of this rejection.

One single criticism can often outweigh hundreds of positive ones. That's why, an author with fifty 5-star reviews, is likely to feel terrible when they receive a single 1-star review. While the author understands the 1-star review isn't a threat to her survival, her authorial brain doesn't. It likely interprets the negative review as a threat to her ego which triggers an emotional reaction.

The fear of rejection can also lead you to over-dramatize events. If your boss criticized you at work, your brain might see the criticism as a threat and you now think, "What if my boss fires me? What if I can't find a job quickly enough and my wife leaves me? What about my kids? What if I can't see them again?"

While you are fortunate to have such a useful survival mechanism, it is also your responsibility to separate real threats from imaginary ones. If you don't, you'll experience unnecessary pain and worry that will negatively impact the quality of your life. To overcome this bias towards negativity, you must reprogram your mind. One of a human being's greatest powers is our ability to use our thoughts to shape our reality and interpret events in a more empowering way. This book will teach you how to do this.

Why your brain's job isn't to make you happy

Your brain's primary responsibility is not to make you happy, but to ensure your survival. Thus, if you want to be happy, you must actively take control of your emotions rather than hoping you'll be happy because it's your natural state. In the following section, we'll discuss what happiness is and how it works.

How dopamine can mess with your happiness

Dopamine is a neurotransmitter that, among other functions, plays a significant role in rewarding certain behaviors. When dopamine releases into specific areas of your brain—the pleasure centers—you get an intense sense of wellbeing similar to a high. This sense of wellbeing is what happens during exercise, when you gamble, have sex, or eat great food.

One of the roles of dopamine is to ensure you look for food so you don't die of starvation, and you search for a mate so you can reproduce. Without dopamine, our species would likely be extinct by now. It's a pretty good thing, right?

Well, yes and no. In today's world, this reward system is, in many cases, obsolete. In the past, dopamine directly linked to our survival, now, it can be stimulated artificially. A great example of this effect is social media, which uses psychology to suck as much time as possible out of your life. Have you noticed all these notifications that pop up regularly? They're used to trigger a release of dopamine so you stay connected, and the longer you stay connected, the more money the services make. Watching pornography or gambling also leads to a release of dopamine which can make these activities highly addictive.

Fortunately, we don't need to act each time our brain releases dopamine. For instance, we don't need to continuously check our Facebook newsfeeds just because it gives us a pleasurable shot of dopamine.

Today's society is selling a version of happiness that can make us *un*happy. We've become addicted to dopamine mainly because of marketers who have found effective ways to exploit our brains. We receive multiple shots of dopamine throughout the day and we love it. But is that the same thing as happiness?

Worse than that, dopamine can create real addictions with severe consequences on our health. Research conducted at Tulane University showed that, when permitted to self-stimulate their pleasure center, participants did it an average of forty times per minute. They chose the stimulation of their pleasure center over food, even refusing to eat when hungry!

Korean, Lee Seung Seop is an extreme case of this syndrome. In 2005, Mr Seop died after playing a video game for fifty-eight hours straight with very little food or water, and no sleep. The subsequent investigation concluded the cause of death was heart failure induced by exhaustion and dehydration. He was only twenty-eight years old.

To take control of your emotions, you must understand the role dopamine plays and how it affects your happiness. Are you addicted to your phone? Are you glued to your TV? Or maybe you spend too much time playing video games. Most of us are addicted to something. For some people it's obvious, but for others, it's more subtle. For instance, you could be addicted to thinking. To better control your emotions, you must recognize and shed the light on your addictions as they can rob you of your happiness.

The 'one day I will' myth

Do you believe that one day you will achieve your dream and finally be happy? It is unlikely to happen. You may (and I hope you will) achieve your goal, but you won't live 'happily ever after.' This thinking is just another trick your mind plays on you.

Your mind quickly acclimates to new situations, which is probably the result of evolution and our need to adapt continually to survive and reproduce. This acclimatization is also probably why the new car or house you want will only make you happy for a while. Once the initial excitement wears off, you'll move on to crave the next exciting thing. This phenomenon is known as 'hedonic adaptation.'

How hedonic adaptation works

Let me share an interesting study that will likely change the way you see happiness. This study, which was conducted in 1978 on lottery winners and paraplegics, was incredibly eye-opening for me. The investigation evaluated how winning the lottery or becoming a paraplegic influence happiness:

The study found that one year after the event, both groups were just as happy as they were beforehand. Yes, just as happy (or unhappy). You can find more about it by watching Dan Gilbert's TED Talk, The Surprising Science of Happiness.

Perhaps you believe that you'll be happy once you've 'made it.' But, as the above study on happiness shows, this is simply not true. No matter what happens to you, your mind works by reverting to your predetermined level of happiness once you've adapted to the new event.

Does that mean you can't be happier than you are right now? No.

What it means is that, in the long run, external events have minimal impact on your level of happiness.

In fact, according to Sonja Lyubomirsky, author of *The How of Happiness*, fifty percent of our happiness is determined by genetics, forty percent by internal factors, and only ten percent by external factors. These external factors include such things as whether we're single or married, rich or poor, and similar social influences.

The influence of external factors is probably way less than you thought. The bottom line is this: Your attitude towards life influences your happiness, not what happens to you.

By now, you understand how your survival mechanism negatively impacts your emotions and prevents you from experiencing more joy and happiness in your life. In the next section, we'll learn about the ego.

To read more visit my author page at:

amazon.com/author/thibautmeurisse

OTHER BOOKS BY THE AUTHORS:

Crush Your Limits: Break Free from Limitations and Achieve Your True Potential

Goal Setting: The Ultimate Guide to Achieving Life-Changing Goals

Habits That Stick: The Ultimate Guide to Building Habits That Stick Once and For All

Master Your Destiny: A Practical Guide to Rewrite Your Story and Become the Person You Want to Be

Master Your Emotions: A Practical Guide to Overcome Negativity and Better Manage Your Feelings

Master Your Focus: A Practical Guide to Stop Chasing the Next Thing and Focus on What Matters Until It's Done

Master Your Motivation: A Practical Guide to Unstick Yourself, Build Momentum and Sustain Long-Term Motivation

Master Your Success: Timeless Principles to Develop Inner Confidence and Create Authentic Success

Master Your Thinking: A Practical Guide to Align Yourself with Reality and Achieve Tangible Results in the Real World

Productivity Beast: An Unconventional Guide to Getting Things Done

The Greatness Manifesto: Overcome Your Fear and Go After What You Really Want

The One Goal: Master the Art of Goal Setting, Win Your Inner Battles, and Achieve Exceptional Results

The Passion Manifesto: Escape the Rat Race, Uncover Your Passion and Design a Career and Life You Love

The Thriving Introvert: Embrace the Gift of Introversion and Live the Life You Were Meant to Live

The Ultimate Goal Setting Planner: Become an Unstoppable Goal Achiever in 90 Days or Less

Upgrade Yourself: Simple Strategies to Transform Your Mindset, Improve

Your Habits and Change Your Life

Success is Inevitable: 17 Laws to Unlock Your Hidden Potential, Skyrocket Your Confidence and Get What You Want From Life

Wake Up Call: How To Take Control Of Your Morning And Transform Your Life

ABOUT THE AUTHOR

THIBAUT MEURISSE

Thibaut Meurisse is a personal development blogger, author, and founder of whatispersonaldevelopment.org. M

Obsessed with self-improvement and fascinated by the power of the brain, his personal mission is to help people realize their full potential and reach higher levels of fulfillment and consciousness.

In love with foreign languages, he is French, writes in English, and lived in Japan for almost ten years.

Learn more about Thibaut at:

amazon.com/author/thibautmeurisse
whatispersonaldevelopment.org
thibaut.meurisse@gmail.com

ACTION GUIDE

Part I. The nature of belief

Chapter 1. What belief is

True belief

Rate yourself on a scale from 1 to 10 for each of the statements below (1 being false, 10 being true):

I know deep down that I can figure things out and eventually will.

0 _____ 10

I developed the ability to remain convinced of that "truth" for months or years

0 _____ 10

I refuse to let my environment stand in the way of your goals.

0 _____ 10

I move through my day with that inner sense of confidence

0 _____ 10

The difference between belief and delusion

Write down below one of your biggest goals or dreams:

My goal:

Now, how delusional are you regarding that goal? In other words, if you keep doing what you're currently doing, how likely are you to achieve that goal (realistically). Write your answer below:

What do you think you would need to do to make sure you reach that goal (or significantly increase the odds you do)?

Chapter 2. The 5 characteristics of belief

#1. Belief is a skill

What are you currently doing to develop more belief in yourself and in your vision? Write two to three specific answers below:

-

-

-

Now, write down what you could be doing to cultivate even more belief:

#2. Belief is neutral

Belief is neutral. Nobody and nothing can prevent you from using your ability to believe to achieve your goals. Knowing that, how will you leverage your power of belief starting today? What will you use it for? Write down your answer below:

#3. Belief is your responsibility

It is your responsibility to believe in yourself. For a moment, close your eyes and let that truth sink in. Realize that you can and will cultivate rock-solid belief over time. Accept the fact that your ability to believe is undeniable.

Now, knowing belief is your responsibility, write down one thing you will do to regain control over your power of belief (for instance, joining a group of like-minded people, distancing yourself from a toxic person or reading biographies from successful people).

To regain control over my power of belief I will:

#4. Belief is available at all time

Your ability to believe can never be taken away from you. Take a moment to notice that ability right now. Realize that, at this very moment, you can choose to believe.

Now, write down what you would do differently, if you were absolutely convinced that the power of belief was available to you at all time:

#5. Belief is a gift you give to the world

If you dramatically increased your level of self-belief, who around you would be positively impacted? Who would be inspired? Write down your answer below:

Chapter 3. The power of belief

Belief can "distorts" reality by:

1. Changing how you think, feel and act, opening doors to countless opportunities that didn't exist before,
2. Turning your subconscious into a powerful ally,
3. Influencing people around you, and
4. Inspiring people.

1. Belief changes how you think, feel and act

Think of one of the most empowering beliefs you could adopt (i.e. something that if you believed would make the biggest positive impact on your life). Write your answer below:

2. Belief turns your subconscious into a powerful ally

How do you think your subconscious could help you make that belief comes true (come up with solutions, lead you to take different actions etc.)

Write down your answer below:

3. Belief influences people around you

How would your new belief affect people around you (if relevant)?

4. Belief inspires people

If you knew that, with your ability to believe, you could see in people more potential than they see in themselves, in what way would you become an inspiration for them? How would you support them? Write down your answer below:

Your thoughts create your reality

Think of one thing you really want to see happening in the future (getting a promotion, finding a better job, traveling overseas etc.)

Now, imagine if that one thing became your single point of focus. Imagine if it were the only thing you could think about. Write down what specific actions you will likely start taking as a result of focusing monomaniacally on that thought.

Specific actions I would likely take:

Your belief determines your results

If you were to rate your current level of self-belief on a scale from 1 (playing it small) to 100 (giving it all), what would it be (Be honest)?

Your current level of self belief:

Now, what you do you want your level of self-belief to be thirty days from now

My level of self-belief in thirty days:

What do you plan on doing to get there? Write down your answers below. Try to be as specific as possible.

Belief makes impossible things possible

For a moment, let go of any limitations other people may be imposing on you right now. Instead, focus on what the absolute best version of yourself could accomplish. Now, what "impossible" things could you make possible in the near future? Write down your answers below:

The size of your thinking determines the size of your accomplishments

What are you thinking about the most these days? Write down your dominant thoughts below:

Imagine you keep having these same thoughts moving forward. Now, extrapolate what's likely to happen in the future and write down your answer below:

Now, is it what you really want? If not, write down a few dominant thoughts you would like to adopt instead:

Confidence vs. arrogance

Write down a few things you could do to appear more confident, perhaps, even to the point of being seen as arrogant (broadcast your desire, stop using words such as "I'll try", "I hope", "I wish" etc.)

Then, experiment with one of these things.

Part II. Identifying your limiting beliefs

Chapter 4. Belief and identity

Think of one major goal you'd like to achieve and write it down below:

Now, write down a few statements that would describe the identity of someone who has already achieved that goal.

Chapter 5. Overcoming your limiting beliefs

Identifying your limiting beliefs

Select the one area of your life you want to focus on the most right now. Consider the following areas: career, family, finance, personal growth, relationships, social life, spirituality. Then, answer the question below.

How come I'm not at a ten out of ten in that area?

You can make excuses or you can make progress

When you tolerate excuses you reduce your field of possibilities. What excuses are you tolerating right now? Write down two to three excuses that if you were let go of would have the biggest positive impact in your life.

-

-

-

Challenging your limiting beliefs

Look at the excuses you wrote down in the previous exercise. Now, ask yourself: are these excuses really true all the time in every circumstance? Or are they merely limiting beliefs you're holding onto?

Finding counter examples in your life

Now select one of your limiting beliefs and answer the following question:

Are my limiting beliefs always true all the time in any circumstance?

Your limiting belief:

The answer is probably no. So, look for examples in your own life that show your limiting beliefs are inaccurate. Write them down below:

Example 1:

Example 2:

Example 3:

Gathering proofs your beliefs are inaccurate

Now, gather case studies that show that these beliefs are likely to be inaccurate. For instance, look for stories of people similar to you who manage to do that thing you find excuses not to do. You can write the case studies you've found using the space below:

Chapter 6. Integrating your new beliefs

Finally, you want to integrate your new beliefs to make them part of your identity. You can do that in several different ways:

- By writing them down and looking at them on a regular basis
- By thinking about them often
- By acting in a way that strengthens them
- By thinking of all the reasons why they are accurate, and/or
- By thinking of all the reasons why *you want* them to be true

Part III. Building foundational beliefs

Chapter 7. The #1 meta-belief that rules them all

Imagine that your thoughts create your reality. If so, what new thoughts could you adopt in order to design a better reality? Write down some of them below:

Chapter 8. Seven core beliefs that will transform your life

Belief #1 — The universe is on your side

Imagine you truly believed that the universe was on your side. If so, what new more empowering interpretation would you give to some of your current life circumstances?

Write down below two to three challenges you're facing and how you perceive them differently if you believe the universe was on your side. For instance, perhaps, there is a lesson for you to learn.

Challenge #1:

New perspective you could adopt:

Challenge #2:

New perspective you could adopt:

Challenge #3:

New perspective you could adopt:

Belief #2 — If others can, so can you

Write down three things other people are doing that you wish you could do too (for instance, speaking a foreign language, delivering speeches, playing an instrument well etc.)

1.

2.

3.

Now, realize that if others can, you can too.

Belief #3 - You can always become better

See yourself as a perpetual learner and understand that becoming better is inevitable.

Write down below all the reasons you can become better:

-

-

-

-

-

-

-

-

-

-

Belief #4 — If you can do something once, you can do it again

- Think of one challenging thing you haven't been able to do (yet).
- Then realize you can do it just one time. And even if you can't right now, at least, you can take one small step in that direction.
- Finally, understand that, if you can do that thing just once, you'll be able to do it again

Belief #5—You can figure things out

You're a natural problem solver who can solve almost any problem you'll ever encounter. You *can* figure things out. So begin to adopt the belief that you can figure things out.

Now, write down one major problem you're currently facing:

Your problem:

Then, write down all the things you could do to solve it. Just write down everything that comes to mind:

-
-
-
-
-
-
-
-
-
-
-
-

Belief #6—Failure is inevitable

To achieve success you'll have to "fail" repeatedly. However, in truth, there isn't such thing as "failure". There is only feedback from reality. So being to change your relationship with failure and see it as feedback. Every time you fail and learn from your failure, you move a little closer from your goal.

Now, write down one big "failure" in your life.

Your failure:

Then, answer the following questions:

What did I learn from it?

What's good about it? What positive things did it lead to? (mindset change, new opportunities, invaluable lessons learned etc.)

Belief #7—Your success is inevitable

Adopt the belief that success is inevitable as you learn to use the power of belief.

Remember:

- You have the ability to use your thoughts to shape your reality
- If others can, you can too
- You can always become better
- If you manage to do something once, you can do it again,
- You're capable enough to figure things out
- Short-term failure is inevitable and leads to long-term success

As such, over a long enough period of time, you can achieve almost anything you desire. So start acting as if your success was inevitable and see how things change for you.

Complete the following sentence: If I believe success was inevitable for me I would:

Part IV. The Belief Formula

Below is a break down of the Belief Formula:

Empowering environment + repeating action + intense desire + willingness to face discomfort = Unshakeable belief

- **Empowering environment.** It is consciously putting yourself in a favorable environment that enables you to perform at your best.
- **Repeated action.** Taking action can solve a lot of problems including a lack of self-confidence. It is what allows you to reinforce your core beliefs so that you can cultivate greater confidence over time
- **Intense desire.** Knowing why you want something gives you the motivation to keep going and persevere during tough times.
- **Willingness to face discomfort.** It's the repeated exposure to fear through concrete action that enables you to get a glimpse of your true nature (i.e. the confident and capable person you inherently are as a human being).

Chapter 9. Empowering environment

1. Mental environment

Reprogramming your mind

What you could do every day to maintain a positive emotional state? Write down your answers below:

Repeating powerful affirmations

Come up with a couple of affirmations you could repeat every day to develop a stronger mindset:

Your affirmations:

-

-

Using the power of visualization

Practice visualization every day when you wake and/or when you go to bed. To begin with, you can focus on one specific feeling or one particular belief you want to adopt.

Remember to follow the simple steps below:

1) **Relax.** As you put yourself in a deep state of relaxation, you'll gain better access to your subconscious.

2) **Visualize what you want.** See your ideal outcome as vividly as possible.

3) **Feel as if you're already there.** Engage your emotions. Get excited about your vision. Feel as if you were already the person you want to be, having the things you want to have.

4) **Keep focusing on what you want.** Repetition is key. Keep visualizing every day as often as you can.

2. Social environment

What type of people do you want to surround yourself with?

Is there acquaintance you'd like to spend more time with? If so write their names below:

Where are you the most likely to find people you want to surround yourself with?

Which relevant groups or forum could you join online?

Which book(s) written by people you want to be like could you read?

Could you create your own tribe? If so, what tribe would that be?

3. Physical environment

What are specific things you could do to improve your physical environment? (removing junk food from your house, prepare your running gears the night before etc.)

Chapter 10. Repeated actions

To boost your confidence, set three tiny goals every day and achieve them consistently for at least 7 days and preferably thirty days.

The power of habits

Below are seven powerful habits you can experiment. Perhaps start with one (or two at most).

1. Setting daily goals
2. Reading your goals every day
3. Meditating
4. Practicing gratitude
5. Consuming motivational books and videos
6. Self-reflecting
7. Exercising daily

How to implement habits that stick

To implement your new habits, you can use the 5 simple steps below:

1. **Define your habits clearly.** Make sure it is measurable so that you know whether you've performed it or not.
2. **Start small.** Make your habit is easy so that you can stick to it long term and build momentum.
3. **Set specific triggers.** Have a specific event or action after which you'll perform your habit. That will prevent you from forgetting about your new habit.
4. **Stack your habits.** Create a chain of habits by implementing a morning ritual for instance.
5. **Undertake a 30-day challenge.** Stick to your new habits for 30 days in a row. This will help you establish your new habits.

Your turn now

Write down three (small) habits you want to implement.

-

-

-

Then, stack them together and stick to them for the next 30 days.

How to take more actions

Select one major goal you're currently working on.

Your goal:

Separate true actions from feel good activities

Now, make a list of the actions you're taking to reach it using the table below

True actions	Feel good activities

Take more true actions

Practice taking more actions that get you tangible results (i.e. true actions).

A good idea is to incorporate them in your morning ritual whenever possible.

Chapter II. Intense desire

Creating a burning desire

Write down a few things you really desire in your life:

-

-

-

-

-

Now, among the things you wrote down in the previous exercise, select the one that excites you the most.

The one thing I want the most:

Energizing your goals

Write down all the benefits you'll gain from achieving that goal. Try to be as specific as possible. Also, make sure that these reasons are linked to some of your core values.

Why I want that thing:

1.

2.

3.

4.

5.

Further energizing your goals

Now, for each benefit you've identified, write down what exactly it would look like and why it matters

Benefit #1:

What it would look like:

Why it matters:

Benefit #2:

What it would look like:

Why it matters:

Benefit #3:

What it would look like:

Why it matters:

Benefit #4:

What it would look like:

Why it matters:

Benefit #5:

What it would look like:

Why it matters:

Chapter 12. Willingness to face discomfort

Select one thing that you believe is impossible for you (or very challenging)

Your impossible thing:

Think of the smallest step you could take in that direction and write it down:

Alternatively, if you can muster the courage, do that impossible thing now.

If needed, get support from people. It could be by having an accountability partner, hiring a coach or joining a group of like-minded people.

Part V. Sustaining belief long-term

Chapter 13. The power of long-term thinking

If you were a long-term thinker what would you start doing differently? Write down your answers below:

Long-term belief vs. temporary self-doubt

Think of one goal you failed to achieve in the past? Now, imagine if you could go back in time and used the power of long-term belief. What would you have done differently?

The power of grit

Envision the worst-case scenarios

Think of your major goal. Now, write down what the worst-case scenarios could be:

-

-

-

-

Determine your threshold for giving up

What could make you give up on that goal? Write down the criteria that would need to be met in order of you to throw in the towel.

-

-

-

-

-

Write down your bullet-proof timeframe

Finally, set a timeframe during which you will commit to work on that goal. For any major goal, you might want to consider giving yourself two to three years.

Your bullet-proof timeframe:

Chapter 14. How to transition from short-term to long-term thinking

To develop your ability to think long term, complete the exercises below:

Creating a long-term vision

Think of a long-term goal or vision you'd like to pursue and write it down below:

Thinking of your long-term goals often

Write this long-term goal/vision and put it somewhere you can see it often

Dedicating time to focus on the big picture

Every week, dedicate at least 15 minutes to think of your long-term goal/vision and assess how well you're doing. Below are some questions you might want to ask yourself:

- What am I satisfied with?
- What do I want or need to improve?
- What can I do differently to speed up my progress?
- If I were to start the week all over again, what would I do differently?
- If I keep doing what I've done this week, will I achieve my long-term goal? If not, what changes do I need to make?

- Is my current strategy the best one possible? If not, how can I refine it to make it even better?
- What are the very few things that generate most of my results? Can I focus more on these things?
- What are all the things that haven't proven to be effective so far? Can I get rid of some of them?
- If I only work on one thing this week/month/year, what would be best in terms of overall progress?

Learning to love the process

Complete the sentence below:

For me, focusing more on the process would mean ...

Letting go of the fear of missing out

Complete the exercises below:

- Write down the area(s) of your life in which you experience fear of missing out.
- Select one specific area or goal and write down all the opportunities that actually exist out there. What are your options? What could you do about it?
- Take a moment to appreciate all the opportunities available to you.

Reminding yourself to be patient

Complete the exercises below:

- Create your own mantras such as "life is a marathon, not a sprint", or simply "be patient". Then think of them often, write them down and/or display them on your desk or on your wall.

- Watch Gary Vee's videos, "Overnight Success" and "People have forgotten the art of patience" on Youtube).

Focus on all the reasons you can be successful

Write down all the reasons why you can be successful. Repeat the same exercise whenever necessary.

Chapter 15. Winning the emotional game

3 key characteristics of negative emotions

1. Negative emotions act as a spell
2. Negative emotions filter your experiences
3. Negative emotions attract more negative emotions

Complete the exercises below:

- Remember a time when everything felt hopeless or gloomy and you didn't believe you could be happy again. Then, realize your negative emotions eventually faded away.
- Think of three current challenges in your life one after the other. How does each make you feel? Now, visualize three things you're grateful for or excited about. Feel better?

- Think of one poor decision you made as a result of negative emotions (anger, hopelessness, frustration et cetera) or positive emotions (joy, euphoria, excitement, et cetera).
- For one full minute give yourself some words of encouragement. Remind yourself that you're doing well, that you have noble intentions and that you're proud of all the things you've accomplished. How does it make you feel?The importance of self-compassion

How to develop self-compassion

7-day self-compassion challenge

For the next seven days refrain from beating yourself up. Talk to yourself using kind words instead.

Changing your self-talk

Choose one day who you'll pay close attention to your self-talk.

Then, rate your self-talk on a scale from 1 to 10, one being extremely negative, ten being extremely positive.

Quality of my self-talk:

0   10
_____

Did you notice anything in particular? (Recurrent thoughts, common threads, specific words etc). Write your comments below:

Now, what could you tell yourself instead in order to build long-term self-confidence?

The four motivators

Remember the four motivators below and use them whenever necessary.

1) Love

A sincere desire to contribute to the world and make a difference in people's lives.

2) Desire

Desire is different from love in that it's not about contributing to other people. It focuses instead on designing the life you want for yourself. It's about living life on your own terms.

3) Pain

Nobody wants to suffer, and we spend a lot of time shying away from pain. When used intelligently, pain can be an effective tool to motivate you when you'd rather do nothing.

4) Ego

Ego can also be a powerful motivator. You can use your desire to be successful, feel loved or prove those who didn't believe in you wrong, to your advantage.

Made in the USA
Las Vegas, NV
23 October 2024

10411807R10118